DATE DUE

MAR 30 1983			

UPI

Printed in USA

D1777203

Operations Auditing in Hospitals

Operations Auditing in Hospitals

Dale L. Flesher
Appalachian State University

Lexington Books
D.C. Heath and Company
Lexington, Massachusetts
Toronto   London

Library of Congress Cataloging in Publication Data

Flesher, Dale L.
 Operations auditing in hospitals.

 Bibliography: p.
 1. Hospitals—Administration. 2 Management audit. 3. Hospitals—Accounting. I. Title.
RA971.F56   658.4'03   75-29936
ISBN 0-669-00363-8

Copyright © 1976 by D.C. Heath and Company.

All rights reserved. No part of this publication may be reproduced or transmitted in any form or by any means, electronic or mechanical, including photocopy, recording, or any information storage or retrieval system, without permission in writing from the publisher.

Published simultaneously in Canada.

Printed in the United States of America.

International Standard Book Number: 0-669-00363-8

Library of Congress Catalog Card Number: 75-29936

Contents

	List of Figures	ix
	Acknowledgments	xi
Chapter 1	**Introduction**	1
	The Research	3
	The Study	5
Chapter 2	**Operations Auditing**	7
	History and Development of Auditing	7
	Internal Auditing	9
	Objectives of Operations Auditing	13
	Sources of Data	16
	Limitations of Operations Auditing	18
	Why an Independent Public Accountant?	18
	Summary	20
Chapter 3	**Hospital Accounting and Auditing**	21
	The 1933 Committee Report	23
	Cost Reimbursement	25
	Hospital Auditing	26
	Operations Auditing	28
	Summary	28
Chapter 4	**Development of an Operations Audit Model**	31
	The Need for a Model	31
	Preliminary Steps	32
	Survey Memorandum	45
	The In-Depth Audit	46
	The Audit Report	46
	The Recommended Operations Audit Model	47
	Summary	47

Chapter 5	Model In-Depth Audits	51
	Patient Census Management (Admissions and Discharges) Department	51
	Personnel Department	54
	Accounting Department	56
	Payroll Department	59
	Purchasing Department	61
	Receiving and Materials Handling Department	64
	Summary	66
Chapter 6	Conclusion	67
	Summary	67
	Procedural Review	68
	Recommendations for Further Study	69
	Appendixes	71
Appendix A	Operations Audit Questionnaire: Patient Census Management Department	73
Appendix B	Operations Audit Questionnaire: Personnel Department	79
Appendix C	Operations Audit Questionnaire: Accounting Department	85
Appendix D	Operations Audit Questionnaire: Payroll Department	91
Appendix E	Operations Audit Questionnaire: Purchasing Department	97
Appendix F	Operations Audit Questionnaire: Receiving and Materials Handling Department	103
Appendix G	Operations Audit Test Cases: Survey Memoranda and Audit Reports	109
Appendix H	Sample Hospital Advisory Services (HAS) Report	113

Notes	117
Bibliography	125
Index	133
About the Author	135

List of Figures

4-1	Operations Audit Model	48
4-2	Operations Audit Model—Specific Sources	49

Acknowledgments

I wish to thank Dale L. Kiefer, Wayne S. Overmyer, Richard Shell, Charles Barngrover, and Milan Karas, all of the University of Cincinnati, for the time they devoted to this project. Professor Overmyer deserves special thanks for the many hours of his time he spent in assisting this researcher.

I particularly wish to express my appreciation to my wife and fellow accountant, Tonya, for her love and understanding during the period when this research project was being conducted.

Appendix H is from the Six-Month National Comparison for the period ending December 31, 1972 and is reprinted here by permission of the American Hospital Association.

Operations Auditing in Hospitals

1 Introduction

Hospitals, a term that is broadly used to designate the institutions where the sick or wounded receive medical treatment, have made considerable progress during the past half century. There are now over 8,000 hospitals in the United States, which thus makes hospital service one of the largest industries in the country.[1] The field of health care is presently the third largest industry in the United States both in terms of contribution to GNP and employment. At one time, a hospital was considered strictly as a charitable organization that was a social requirement of every community. Today, however, hospitals are expected to be run on a sound business basis similar to any other industry. The increased use of hospitalization insurance, workmen's compensation programs, and Medicare have all played a role in bringing the hospital industry up to date in its business practices. The future possibility of some form of national health insurance program promises to place even more strains on the management practices of hospital administrators.

Hospital administration is a rather complex business. A hospital has certain characteristics that make it similar to a hotel, a restaurant, a leasing company, a gift shop, a school, a drug store, and numerous other types of businesses. In addition, a hospital is still partially a charitable organization and must care for patients whether or not the patients are able to pay for the services rendered. An additional factor that makes hospital administration difficult is the question of who really is in command of a hospital. It is often argued that the hospital administrator (president) has very little say in running the hospital. Instead, it is often felt that the individual doctors (who are, in most cases, not even employees of the hospitals) have more control than the hospital administrator. Additionally, the board of trustees (usually a group of civic-minded townsfolk) have some say in how a hospital is to be run.

Given the complicated nature of the hospital organization, the problems peculiar to the industry, and the fact that the majority of hospitals are considered to be nonprofit organizations, it is easy to understand that there are problems of measuring managerial efficiency in such institutions. In a normal business, a department's contribution margin can be used to determine managerial effectiveness, but the requirement to serve welfare cases negates that method for hospitals.

For these reasons, it seems that the technique of operations auditing (often referred to as managerial auditing, operational auditing, functional auditing, or even comprehensive auditing[2]) would be especially appropriate for reviewing hospital business operations. The American Management Association has expressed a preference for the term operations auditing,[3] which, accordingly, will be used throughout this volume to refer to this reviewing or examination process.

The operations audit is a thorough examination with the objective of appraising managerial organization, performance, and techniques. It might be considered as an attempt at constructive criticism. The auditor attempts to determine the extent to which organization objectives have been achieved. Operations auditing is a control technique that provides management with a method for evaluating the effectiveness of operating procedures and internal controls. The operations audit is the broadest type of audit and covers all of the functions of a business. One author defined this managerial type of audit in the following manner:

Operational auditing is using common sense, or logical audit techniques, with management perspective, and applying them to company objectives, operations, controls, communications and information systems. The auditor is more concerned with the who, what, when, where, why and how of running an efficient and profitable business than just the accounting and financial aspects of the business functions.[4]

The audit report resulting from an operations audit consists primarily of pointing out where problems exist or emphasizing the absence of problems. The auditor does not necessarily recommend what the improvements should be; the objective is only to point out the problem areas.[5] Someone else is expected to find the solution to the problem. This "someone else" may be either the internal management of the department with the problem or an outside consultant, such as the management advisory services department of a CPA firm or other management consultants.

Any qualified auditor may perform an operations audit. Traditionally, operations audits have been performed primarily by internal auditors and government audit agencies. The General Accounting Office (GAO) has been particularly effective in this area. A small firm without an internal audit staff (a group that would include the majority of hospitals) would find it more economical to use outside auditors for performance of operations audits. Most large CPA firms (The Big Eight) have operations audit divisions,[6] and many regional CPA firms have recognized the potential of such engagements.[7]

Since hospitals are not at present generally considered as profitable ventures and there are so many problems in determining the effectiveness of hospital management, it seems only appropriate that operations auditing would be a major contribution toward improving administrative practices in most hospitals. Since many hospitals can not afford to maintain a full-time internal audit staff, one alternative is for these hospitals to utilize the services of independent public accounting firms. Public accounting firms should be willing to provide such services at nominal charges for two reasons. First, such work can be scheduled at any time during the year, which would thus enable the accounting firm to make more profitable use of slack periods, and second, the operations audit function could be an adjunct area to the management services division. If the audit client needed assistance in solving any problems noted in the operations audit report, the logical place to look for help would be the management services department of the same accounting firm. In fact, the CPA firm might find it advisable to place knowledgable members of the management services staff on the audit team when an operations audit is being conducted.[8] Not only would the audit be benefited by the expertise of the management services people, but the firm would benefit from having the management services staff in continuing contact with the client. There is currently no consensus among CPA firms as to which staff members perform operations audits. Some firms use only auditing personnel, some use only management services staff members, and some firms use a group composed of both types of employees.[9]

The Research

The objectives of the research conducted as part of this study are basically four in number:

1. To review the literature relating to the history and the development of hospital accounting and auditing in the United States.
2. To review the development of operations auditing and explore its application in various aspects of industry and government with the goal of applying such data to the audit of a hospital.
3. To discuss the problems and implications of independent public accountants applying operations auditing techniques to nonprofit[a] hospitals—that is, those hospitals that are classified as charitable under Section 501(c)(3) of the Internal Revenue Code of 1954.
4. To propose a generalized operations audit model (complete with audit program and audit questionnaires) for operations audits of small (under 150 beds), nonteaching general hospitals that serve general medical and surgical patients, maternity patients, and children.

The first step in meeting this last goal—preparing an operations audit program and model—was to determine what problems exist in hospital business offices. This was accomplished by questioning hospital controllers, department heads,

---
[a]Nonprofit is a misnomer, however, since these hospitals may earn a profit, but such income is not subject to federal income tax. (The income is never distributed, but is used for future funding; and the hospital must have a policy of admitting the poor, the distressed, and the underprivileged along with individuals who are capable of paying for hospital service.)

and independent certified public accountants. A one-page questionnaire was sent to approximately 25 hospital controllers, 150 department heads, and a small number of CPAs for each of six departments typically found in hospital business operations. The questionnaire consisted of an open question regarding what the individual felt were the five key problems in a particular department. The open question form was used since its primary quality is in the obtaining of new ideas, and that was what was being attempted at that stage of the research. The respondents were selected in the following manner:

1. Controllers were selected in a simple random sample from all institutional members of the North Carolina chapter of the Hospital Financial Management Association (HFMA), which consists of 157 members.

2. Department heads at all of the above hospitals received questionnaires. The questionnaires were sent to the department heads of the department being studied (for example, only payroll department heads received questionnaires relating to payroll departments).

3. Independent certified public accountants were hand-selected on a non-random basis from CPAs who had had experience in auditing or providing management services to hospitals. A random sample was not feasible because of the small population size and the lack of a listing of the population.

The data obtained from these open questionnaires were supplemented by ideas obtained from reviewing the literature. No attempt was made to apply different weightings to the responses of the different groups. All ideas were considered to be of equal merit at that stage of the research. All ideas obtained from these four sources (controllers, department heads, CPAs, and the literature) were compiled into operations audit questionnaires for each of the six departments (purchasing, receiving and materials handling, personnel, accounting, payroll, and patient census management).

These operations audit questionnaires were then sent out to hospital department heads in the small (under 150 beds) general hospitals in the state of North Carolina with instructions for the department heads to rate each question on a graphic rating scale of the semantic differential type. The following ratings were used: "Not Important," 0; "Of Minor Importance," 1; "Important," 2; "Very Important," 3. The overall average rating given to each question in the audit program was tabulated and those that resulted in an average of 1.0 or higher were considered by the author to be valuable enough to be included in the final program and model (the major objective of this work). Only hospital department heads were used for this final stage of the research with the assumption being that these individuals are best qualified to recognize problems in their own departments. The response rate for the questionnaires, which were sent to six department heads at each of the 84 small general hospitals in the state, was as follows: accounting, 35.7 percent; patient census management, 41.7 percent; payroll, 46.4 percent; personnel, 53.6 percent; purchasing, 53.6 percent; and receiving and materials handling, 39.3 percent.

The most important responses formed the basis for the audit model that was deductively reasoned from the questionnaires. A groundwork is provided for each step of the model including both the preliminary and depth stages. Finally, the resulting model and program were then tested by utilizing them in the audits of two small hospitals. (See Appendix G for the results of those audits.)

Because the extent of a hospital organization is so complex, it was necessary to limit the scope of the program to that of a small hospital. The type of hospital to which it applies is one that does not engage in funded research and is not considered as a teaching hospital. The hospital type is of the general medical and surgical class as opposed to the special illness type.

Since it was assumed that such hospitals do not have internal audit staffs, the audit techniques and programs are discussed from the viewpoint of the independent public accountant. There does not appear to be any reason, at least in the opinion of this writer, why the model could not be equally useful to an internal audit staff if such a staff exists.

Also, it was assumed that the auditor should not be expected to appraise the technical skills of specialists such as pharmacists, doctors, x-ray technologists, anesthesiologists, or other technical professionals. The auditor's major contribution is in the area of appraisal of the manner in which an activity or operation is administered and whether definitions of objectives and their conformity to sound business principles have been made and communicated to all involved parties. Within the framework of this study, the operations audit is performed *for management.* Although there have been recommendations that audit reports relating to managerial performance should be sent to stockholders as is done in Finland and Sweden,[10] such reports to third parties are not contemplated here. Therefore, there is no question of the auditor having any liability to third parties.

The Study

In line with the objectives of the research, the goals of the study, as presented in this volume, include the following:

1. To make public accountants more aware of the potentialities of operations auditing, a function that is often considered to be only a tool of the internal audit staff and government audit agencies.
2. To make hospital management more aware not only of the potentialities of operations auditing on a continuing basis but also the benefits that can be derived from such an undertaking.
3. To provide an audit model that will serve as a useful framework for an operations audit of a hospital. (The model includes a usable audit program, complete with questionnaires, for use by public accountants in an operations audit of a nonprofit hospital.)

Only a small portion of the study presented here is historical. The major part of the work concerns accounting and auditing problems encountered in implementing an operations audit for a hospital. In addition to this introduction, this volume contains five additional chapters briefly outlined as follows:

Chapter 2, Operations Auditing, discusses the history, development, and scope of operations, or performance auditing. The sources of information consist primarily of a review of the literature of accounting.

Chapter 3, Hospital Accounting and Auditing, covers the development of the traditional financial audit of the hospital accounting function. The need for a more extensive audit of hospitals is examined. Again, the literature of accounting is relied upon, along with that of hospital management.

Chapter 4, Development of an Operations Audit Model, explains the steps that are necessary in performing an operations audit at a hospital. An audit model is provided in order to give a framework for hospital operations auditing. The audit model is analogous to the Mautz and Sharaf model as postulated in *The Philosophy of Auditing*.[11] Naturally, the operations audit model for a hospital will be much more specific than the work of Mautz and Sharaf since it relies on the earlier work and is aimed at a single industry rather than simply at auditing in general. A deductive methodology was employed utilizing operations audit data from other industries coupled with knowledge obtained from hospital department heads.

Chapter 4 is intended not only to be descriptive of the audit, but to justify the steps that are being taken in the audit. For example, an auditor during the physical tour stage could observe that a new patient has been admitted to a room where the bed is not made (or worse yet, where the bed has been removed). This would be a very minor problem but is no way to increase the patient's confidence in the competence of the hospital personnel. There are several steps that could be taken to solve the problem if only it is brought to the attention of the admissions department. Another problem is with respect to discharge of patients. Typically, most patients are discharged during the two-hour period prior to noon, which often results in long lines in the hospital corridor. Solutions to this problem could include "floating" employees from other departments, use of part-time employees only, or elimination of the requirement that all patients must be formally discharged.

Chapter 5, Model In-Depth Audits, discusses generalized audit questionnaires for use in various hospital departments once the preliminary audit has been completed. Some readers may find this chapter to be incomplete since certain departments may not exist in all hospitals and are thus not included in this study. The departments for which audit programs were prepared are those that are believed to exist in all hospitals regardless of size. These areas include purchasing, receiving and materials handling, personnel, accounting, payroll, and patient census management (admissions and discharges).

Chapter 6, Conclusion, summarizes the implications of the preceding chapters, reviews the model operations audit program, and presents some topics for further research in the area of hospital business operations.

2 Operations Auditing

History and Development of Auditing

> The company auditor, whose job once was confined to pouring over financial ledgers, is now becoming a combination private detective, credit sleuth, cost-cutter and all-round trouble shooter.
>
> Auditors who work for corporations still check books for errors or signs of chicanery. But they also are moving into new areas of responsibility that bear little relation to their traditional tasks. They are reviewing price policies for possible antitrust violations, investigating outside activities of company officers to spot conflicts of interest, checking credit of suppliers, customers and potential merger partners and roaming plants and offices in search of inefficiency.[1]

As the above quotation from a *Wall Street Journal* article suggests, the concept of an audit has changed in recent years. No longer are the journals, ledgers, and supporting documents the sole subject of the auditors' inquiry. This latest extension of the auditors' role is only a continuation of the types of changes that have dominated the auditing profession throughout the twentieth century.

Prior to the turn of the twentieth century, the major duty of the auditor was the detection of fraud.[2] These audits were usually quite detailed and involved review of almost all transactions for a period. The employment of an independent public accountant by a firm was often looked upon by the public as an indication that there was something wrong with the company since the public accountant was normally associated with fraud, losses, and other irregularities.[3]

The mergers of the late 1890s and early 1900s led to greater employment of public accountants since both parties to a merger wanted to be certain that the combination would be an equitable one for all concerned. The management services aspect of public accounting also arose at this time since, after performing an audit prior to an impending merger, the public accountant usually received the opportunity to design the accounting system for the new firm after the merger.[4]

It was not until 1912 that the detection of fraud and errors really lost their position as the major objectives of an audit. It was then that checking the fairness of financial statements assumed the major role in an audit. Montgomery stated in the first edition of his own auditing textbook (he had previously edited the American edition of Dicksee's auditing text) the following:

In what might be called the formative days of auditing students were taught that the chief objects of an audit were: (1) [t]he detection or prevention of fraud; (2) [t]he detection or prevention of errors; but in recent years there has been a decided change in the demand and in the service. That is to say, the financiers and business men who originally retained professional auditors to look for fraud or errors have enlarged their demands and now require a vastly broader and more important class of work, which those auditors who have advanced in skill and knowledge have been able to understand and perform. We must therefore relegate the former "chief objects" to a subordinate position without in any way depreciating their importance.[5]

Although this was a significant change in the concept of auditing, it was not until the mid-1930s, when such audits became compulsory for a large number of companies, that the full impact became felt. Corporate management was still reluctant to employ public accountants even in the early 1930s because of the early stigma that audits by public accountants were evidence of fraud. One author, who advocated compulsory audits, tried to emphasize the fact that audits were not designed to discover fraud or errors, but were to encourage managers to have policies by which they could justify their actions:

Let us have light—at least enough light so that ownership may know what is being done with its property. If certain operations can not stand publicity, how can we be so certain that they are truly for the best interests of ownership? Officers of banks and holding companies who know that the details of their portfolios will be published, corporate executives who know that their stockholders will be fully informed of their acts, will be powerfully moved to establish supportable policies the soundness of which will be revealed by audit. Thus the entire body of ownership, not merely those persons who are astute enough to read between the lines of obscure or equivocastatements, will be benefited.[6]

The development of the concept of auditing as performed by the independent public accountant advanced very little in the thirty years following the passage of the first securities act in 1933. This is not to say, however, that there were not many advances in auditing during the period. The advances, though, were more procedural than conceptual. Although the final objectives of the public accountant had not changed, the method of achieving those objectives did change.

The first formal acknowledgement by the American Institute of Certified Public Accountants (AICPA) of public accountants' performing audits for some reason other than giving an opinion as to the fairness of financial statements came in 1963 in Statement on Auditing Procedure No. 33.[7] That publication included a chapter entitled "Special Reports." Although the chapter did not mention such engagements as management audits, it did discuss various reports that were prepared for limited purposes. For the first time, it was recognized that public accountants gave opinions on something more than just financial statements. That same chapter also included a section on the auditing of governmental units and nonprofit organizations, which was an acknowledgement of the use of the audit for something other than the benefit of investors. It was becoming ever more noticeable that the role and duties of the independent public accountant was growing broader.

Internal Auditing

Historically, the concept of internal auditing is considered to be of much more recent vintage than that of auditing by external accountants. A form of internal auditing even existed among the manor houses of England during the Middle Ages in that the lord of the manor made annual audits of his managers.[8] Accounting historians often discount these audits when discussing the development of internal auditing since the auditor was really the proprietor who was merely trying to keep up with his own business. More commonly, the railroad industry is usually credited with being the first employers of internal auditors. It was during the latter part of the nineteenth century that these first legitimate internal auditors became commonplace. The title applied to these employees was "traveling auditors," and their duty was to visit the railroad's ticket agents and determine that all monies were properly accounted for. In Germany, the large Krupp Company apparently employed some type of internal audit staff at least as early as 1875 since there is a company audit manual dated January 17, 1875.[9]

Although the roots of internal auditing do date back into the nineteenth century, the real growth did not occur in the United States until the early part of the twentieth century with the growth of the large corporate form of business:

The principal factor in its emergence was the extended span of control faced by management in concerns employing thousands of people and conducting operations from widespread locations. Defalcations and improperly maintained accounting records were obvious problems under these circumstances, and the growth in the volume of transactions presaged a substantial bill for public accounting services for the business that endeavored to solve the problem by continuing the traditional form of audit by the public accountant.[10]

The importance of company size on the employment of internal auditors is further demonstrated by a recent study that showed that among those companies who employed internal auditors, the average ratio of number of internal auditors to number of other employees was 1 to 769.[11]

The objectives of the early internal auditors were primarily built around the protection of company assets. The National Industrial Conference Board's study of internal auditing explained the early motives as follows:

Protection of company assets and detection of fraud were the principal objectives. Consequently, the auditors concentrated most of their attention on examinations of financial records and on the verification of assets that were most easily misappropriated. A popular idea among management people a generation ago was that the main purpose of an auditing program was to serve as a psychological deterrent against wrongdoing by other employees.[12]

That same study recognized the fact that the internal auditor of yesteryear did not perform the same duties as does the modern day internal auditor. Additionally, there was no need for the pioneer internal auditor to perform all of the functions that are handled by today's internal auditors.

In less complicated times, of course, management frequently maintained control over company operations by personal supervision. There were not so many levels of authority separating policy makers from production workers, and demands on senior executives' time were neither so numerous nor so urgent. The need had not yet arisen to adapt the internal auditing function to the requirements of an elaborate management control system.[13]

In reality, the old concept of internal auditing can be compared to a form of insurance. The major objective was to discover fraud much more quickly than it could be discovered by a public accountant during an annual audit. The modern concept of internal auditing is that of an "arm of management." No longer is the internal auditor strictly a policeman. The modern internal auditor is an integral link in the management process.

Perhaps the Institute of Internal Auditors was able to best describe the broad role of internal auditing with its 1957 *Statement of Responsibilities of the Internal Auditor:*

Nature of Internal Auditing

Internal auditing is an independent appraisal activity within an organization for the review of accounting, financial and other operations as a basis for service to management. It is a managerial control, which functions by measuring and evaluating the effectiveness of other controls.

Objective and Scope of Internal Auditing

The over-all objective of internal auditing is to assist all members of management in the effective discharge of their responsibilities, by furnishing them with objective analyses, appraisals, recommendations and pertinent comments concerning the activities reviewed. The internal auditor, therefore, should be concerned with any phase of business activity wherein he can be of service to management. The attainment of this over-all objective of service to management should involve such activities as:

    Reviewing and appraising the soundness, adequacy and application of accounting, financial and operating controls.

    Ascertaining the extent of compliance with established policies, plans and procedures.

    Ascertaining the extent to which company assets are accounted for, and safeguarded from, losses of all kinds.

Ascertaining the reliability of accounting and other data developed within the organization.

Appraising the quality of performance in carrying out assigned responsibilities.[14]

In a recent book on the subject of internal auditing, Sawyer particularly emphasizes the management services and management auditing aspects of the occupation,[15] and an article by the same author tends to indicate that management auditing and modern internal auditing are virtually synonymous phrases.[16] Although this writer realizes that there has been a great change in the duties of the internal auditor during the past decade, there is some doubt as to whether the above phrases are as nearly synonymous as Sawyer likes to believe.

The 1963 study by the National Industrial Conference Board included a survey of 177 companies as to the principal objectives of the companies' internal auditing programs. The five primary objectives were as follows:

1. Determine the adequacy of the system of internal control.
2. Investigate compliance with company policies and procedures.
3. Verify the existence of assets, see that proper safeguards for assets are maintained and prevent or discover fraud.
4. Check on the reliability of the accounting and reporting system.
5. Report findings to management and recommend corrective action where necessary.[17]

These primary objectives were followed by several secondary objectives of internal auditing:

1. Aid in promoting accounting efficiency.
2. Provide a training ground for personnel.
3. Supplement the work of the public accountant and cooperate with them on the annual audit.
4. Appraise personnel performance.
5. Investigate compliance with rules of regulatory agencies.
6. Assist in profit improvement activities.
7. Provide general assistance to management.
8. Assist in instituting new procedures.[18]

It is interesting to note that the objectives of appraising personnel performance, assisting in profit improvement activities, providing general assistance to management, and assisting in the institution of new procedures were all included in the list of secondary objectives. Yet, these would all be considered an aspect of managerial or operations auditing. Perhaps another study is needed on the principal objectives of internal auditing to determine whether the principal objectives have really changed during the past decade or whether internal auditors are only fooling themselves.

At this point, it is not really important how widespread the practice of management auditing is by internal auditors. The important thing is that in some firms and governmental agencies, the internal auditor is viewed as an aid rather than as a policeman.

Various governmental audit agencies have led in the movement toward the modernization of internal auditing procedures. The General Accounting Office (GAO), particularly, has played a major role in broadening the role of the auditor. That organization's publication, *Standards for Audit of Governmental Organizations, Programs, Activities and Functions*, explains the metamorphosis in the following manner:

Accompanying this increased complexity in the relationship among the various levels of government has been an increased demand for information about government programs. Public officials, legislators, and the general public want to know whether governmental funds are handled properly and in compliance with existing laws and whether governmental programs are being conducted efficiently, effectively, and economically. They also want to have this information provided, or at least concurred in, by someone who is not an advocate of the program but is independent and objective.

This demand for information has widened the scope of governmental auditing so that such auditing no longer is a function concerned primarily with financial operations. Instead, governmental auditing now is also concerned with whether governmental organizations are achieving the purposes for which programs are authorized and funds are made available, are doing so economically and efficiently, and are complying with applicable laws and regulations.[19]

The auditing standards advocated in that publication apply to all audits relating to government activities whether performed by internal auditors of federal, state, or local governments, or by independent public accountants.

Basically, the recommended standards encompass all of those standards that have been adopted by the AICPA for use in audits to express an opinion on the fairness of financial statements. Governmental audits, however, should go a step beyond those standards and procedures that are applicable to audits of financial statements.

However, the interests of many users of reports on government audits are broader than those that can be satisfied by audits performed to establish the credibility of financial reports. To provide for audits that will fulfill these broader interests, the standards in this statement include the essence of those prescribed by the American Institute of Certified Public Accountants and additional standards for audits of a broader scope as will be explained subsequently.[20]

The scope of a governmental audit (either an audit of a governmental agency or an audit for a government agency) is composed of three elements. These are:

1. *Financial and compliance*—determines (a) whether financial operations are properly conducted, (b) whether the financial reports of an audited entity are presented fairly, and (c) whether the entity has complied with applicable laws and regulations.

2. *Economy and efficiency*—determines whether the entity is managing or utilizing its resources (personnel, property, space, and so forth) in an economical and efficient manner and the causes of any inefficiencies or uneconomical practices, including inadequacies in management information systems, administrative procedures, or organizational structure.
3. *Program results*—determines whether the desired results or benefits are being achieved, whether the objectives established by the legislature or other authorizing body are being met, and whether the agency has considered alternatives which might yield desired results at a lower cost.[21]

The typical definition of an audit would not include elements 2 and 3. The fairness of financial reports is the primary objective of corporate audits by independent public accountants. The public accountant engaged for his first government audit would find such an engagement to be an almost entirely new experience due to the operations audit requirements. The employment of public accountants for government audits is not at all uncommon. Illinois, for instance, uses public accountants for auditing almost all state agencies.[22]

Not only was the GAO innovative in the scope of its audits, but it has also been quite successful in meeting the objectives for which the broadened scope was intended.[23] The successes of the GAO auditors have been publicly reported in newspapers and in the GAO reports being made available to the public. As a result, internal auditors in industry have taken steps to broaden the scope of their own audits. Thus, the concept of operations auditing is becoming more and more common among internal audit staffs everywhere. The latest edition of one leading auditing textbook states:

Internal auditing activities fall into two major categories: (1) financial and (2) operational or management auditing.[24]

Although there may be some question as to how widespread the practice of operations auditing is among internal auditors, there is no doubt but what the practice is increasing just as operations audits by public accountants are increasing.

Objectives of Operations Auditing

Operations auditing is known by many names. It appears in the literature as operational auditing, management auditing, performance auditing, systems auditing, efficiency auditing, and a few others. Some authors feel that operations auditing is synonymous with internal auditing,[25] but these are individuals who view internal auditing from a modernistic viewpoint.

The literature reflects a wide variety of impressions and ideas relating to operations auditing. As might be expected with a concept bearing many different names, there have been a variety of definitions offered explaining the purposes and objectives of operations auditing. These definitions have ranged from the extreme of "Management auditing is characterized more by a state of mind than by distinctive methods,"[26] to the other extreme of "Management auditing is an audit which results in a statement of opinion by a CPA with regard to the performance of the management function."[27] The authors of one article even attempted to develop the underlying postulates of the theory of management auditing as it might be performed when merely an extension of the annual financial audit.[28]

There are two reasons for not accepting the definition that relates to the CPA giving an opinion on the performance of management. First, there are no objective and generally accepted measurement standards for determining the efficiency of management. Second, the CPA would be exposed to an unprecedented degree of liability to third parties if he were to attempt to give opinions on various human qualities.

Other published definitions of operations auditing that help to explain the concept as it is used here include the following:

Operational auditing has been described as "what the manager would do himself if he only had time for it and knew how" and as "the shadow of the boss." It is a logical extension of management's responsibility for the success of the organization. Its purpose is to determine whether a given operation, activity, function or program is being conducted in a manner in keeping with management's proscribed procedures, policies and objectives and with the demand for economy, efficiency and effectiveness.[29]

Operations auditing is a technique for regularly and systematically appraising unit or function effectiveness against corporate and industry standards by utilizing personnel who are not specialists in the area of study with the objectives of assuring a given management that its aims are being carried out and/or identifying conditions capable of being improved.[30]

The most important thing to appreciate is that there is no such thing as an operational audit. It is a question of approach and scope—the audit techniques are the same.[31]

A systematic, comprehensive, critical and constructive examination and appraisal of the organization structure, management practices and methods conducted by an external independent person(s).[32]

Operations auditing is a review and appraisal of the efficiency and effectiveness of operations and operating procedures. It carries with it the responsibility to discover and inform top management of operating problems, but its chief purpose is assisting management to solve problems by recommending realistic courses of action.[33]

This last definition is not totally acceptable for purposes of this research because of the phrases stating that the audit findings should include specific recommendations and courses of action. Although many authors have defined operations auditing as both a problem-finding and problem-solving tool, the most recent works on the topic have emphasized the fact that the tool is useful only to determine what problems exist. There is nothing new about trying to solve problems; it is the technique of trying to find problems that is of more recent vintage. The operations auditor does not offer suggestions as to how problems might be solved.[34] The job of operations auditing is finished when the problems have been located, identified, and defined. The development of solutions is the job of management, management consultants, or the management services department of a CPA firm. The solving of identified problems is not a new concept; the systematic search for problems and creating opportunities for their solution is new.

Most practical definitions of operations auditing are quite lengthy. The following quotation from an unidentified company's procedures manual is illustrative of the steps sometimes taken to explain operations auditing to employees:

The operational audit evolves somewhat naturally as an extension of the financial audit, going beyond that generally considered the accounting function; it deals with nonfinancial activities that sooner or later are quantitatively expressed in the financial records of the company. A few illustrations of an operational audit are shown below.
   Appraising compliance with policies and procedures.
   Reviewing purchasing practices.
   Reviewing general housekeeping conditions and plant safety standards.
   Reviewing production and scrap reporting processes.
   In essence, operational audits approach how and why things are done, and attempt to measure that which is actually happening against performance standards.
   This takes into focus a much broader plane than financial auditing and becomes a great deal more complex, requiring considerable cooperation among the individuals involved.[35]

Of course, not everyone is supportive of the concept of operations auditing. One corporate finance director stated that the "management audit would seem to be the latest in the series of cure-all packages thrust upon unwary industrialists by well-meaning academics or more commercial profit-seekers."[36]

Despite a few critics, operations auditing does fill a need as a valuable management tool. As business and government have grown increasingly larger, management has found it increasingly difficult to keep informed in all areas under its responsibility. Traditional sources of managerial information do not fully meet the needs of management in large organizations:

Central to the whole concept of operations auditing is the idea that, if they are to operate incisively and creatively, managers need some kind of early warning system for the detection of potentially destructive problems and opportunities for improvement. That is, modern business has had to develop ways to anticipate and cope with the heightened risks and more sophisticated resources involved in reaching its objectives. Operations auditing is one of those ways.[37]

With the use of operations auditing, management can maintain its total effectiveness despite the increased complexity of organizations and the constantly increasing demands on management's time. Admittedly, a manager could perform operations auditing activities himself, but most managers are so busy in implementation of policies that there is little time left to make adequate readings of department positions or directions.

The most distinguishing difference between the traditional financial audit and the operations audit is the scope of the engagement. The traditional audit has the objective of determining the fairness of financial statements with a great emphasis on the internal control of the firm. The operations audit includes a review of the objectives of the company or organization, the environment within which it operates, as well as its operating policies, personnel, and even its physical facilities. The operations auditor will use a greater variety of audit tools to obtain the evidence necessary to fulfill the objectives of the audit.

Sources of Data

The sources of the operations auditor's data include a physical tour of the plant or department, interviews in each functional area with the use of management and operational control questionnaires, and financial analysis work.

An operations audit normally begins with an orientation meeting with high level management to discuss the scope of the audit, the reason for the audit, and the broad policies of the company or organization. This orientation meeting is then followed by a preliminary audit of the firm. The preliminary audit usually includes a physical tour of all facilities and interviews in each functional area (or at least those functional areas that might economically benefit from an intensive operations audit effort). The real purpose of the preliminary survey is to determine what departments might benefit most from an in-depth audit. Occasionally, the preliminary audit might be eliminated because the firm's management already knows what departments need to be audited in depth. In practice, only the one or two departments that appear to have the greatest number of problems are audited. It should be remembered that operations audits are not mandatory, and such audits must be justified on the basis of the cost/benefit ratio. Therefore, the auditor must necessarily limit his study to the areas where the most benefits can be gained.

Once the preliminary audit has been completed, the auditor should prepare an audit report (often called a survey memorandum), but only for his own use. The survey memorandum should not be submitted to anyone since it is based on inconclusive evidence. The only reason to have a survey memorandum is to enable the auditor to collect his thoughts prior to selecting a particular department or functional area to be audited further. Although the preliminary audit may indicate problems in a particular area, the auditor normally has not done sufficient work to be certain of that fact, nor does he know the causes of these problems.

Once the preliminary audit and survey memorandum have been completed, the auditor selects a department or area for an in-depth audit. There are three broad sources of information that the auditor should obtain during the in-depth audit. These are people, internal documentation, and direct observation.[38]

The people working in the department being audited are the primary source of audit data. This phase of gathering information involves a well-conducted interview campaign as well as the use of a questionnaire. The investment of time in developing a good questionnaire is the most significant aspect of operations auditing, since its use insures that audit coverage is complete and that all audits are similar in scope. The questionnaire should be used with numerous respondents to obtain multiple answers to the same questions. This step is not a wasteful one in that different individuals may not view things in the same manner and the auditor is more apt to unearth the truth about a situation when several viewpoints are obtained.

The internal documentation of a department that an operations auditor should obtain includes such items as procedural manuals, organization charts, flow charts, recruiting brochures, advertisements, financial statements, budgets, and variance reports.

Direct observation is a useful tool in that it can unearth problems that could not be determined in any other manner, or problems that employees are trying to hide or of which they are not aware. Additionally, observation provides a source of examples that are useful in illustrating general conclusions.[39]

Once the in-depth audit of an organizational unit has been completed, it should be followed by an exit interview with personnel from the unit being audited.[40] A discussion of the audit results will benefit both the auditor and the employees whose department was audited. The employees get a head start on solving the problems that have been identified and the auditor gets another opportunity to test his findings before filing his final report. In fact, a rough draft of the final audit report should be available for discussion with the department head. Although there will often be disagreement as to how critical some problems are, such conflicting views may add additional insight into the problem areas.

The end product of an operations audit is a formal, written report to the management of the organization. The report should detail what problems have been found. The purpose of the report is to advise management as to areas where the organization can take corrective action. Therefore, the report should include numerous examples, charts, graphs, and schedules. It is even advisable in some cases to include in the report a section for the comments of the managers in the units audited (usually those obtained during the exit interview).

Limitations of Operations Auditing

Operations auditing will not solve all problems; operations auditing has its limitations. "The principal constraints are time, knowledge, and cost."[41] Time is a limiting factor because management must learn about problems quickly enough to do something about them. Therefore, it is imperative that operations audits be performed with sufficient regularity to insure that major problems do not become entrenched within the organization.

A lack of knowledge is the most commonly publicized constraint of operations auditing. It is inherently impossible for operations auditors to be expert in all areas of business that need to be audited, and as a result, operations auditors are typically more fully trained in auditing procedures than in what is being audited. For this reason, then, CPA firms have become involved in operations auditing. Nevertheless, since the audit is conducted by individuals who are not technically qualified in the area being audited, the results must necessarily be limited to major problems.

Although the concept of operations auditing is still not uniform among all accountants (a limitation in itself), the limitations of the concept are not so great as to make it a useless tool. In fact, for the majority of organizations, operations auditing can be a valuable addition to the management process.

Why an Independent Public Accountant?

There is some question as to who should perform operations audits. The first problem is whether the audits should be performed by someone within the organization or by someone external to the organization. Secondly, should operations audits be performed by accountants or by some other professional group? The question of internal auditor versus external auditor is partially related to the size of the organization. Many firms could not afford to employ a full-time operations auditor. Therefore, these firms must rely on outsiders to perform operations audits. This solves the problem of the small and medium-sized firms, but what about the large firms that can afford to hire a full-time operations audit staff? Is there any advantage to large firms in hiring outside auditors to perform operations audits? Some authorities apparently believe that there is value for even the large firm to hire outside auditors:

I have known many instances where internal auditors have made truly excellent suggestions for achieving improvements. For any one of several practical obstacles—possibly personal politics or the general unwillingness to change on the part of other company officials—such suggestions may not have been implemented. The outside auditors, by virtue of their independence and objectivity, can repeat and reinforce these suggestions.[42]

Even a recent edition of *Forbes* magazine discussed the problem in the editor's "Fact and Comment" section:

Why do corporate managers tell all to outside management consultants and clam up with in-house talent trying to do the same sort of analysis? Principally because the outside experts are not seeking to replace all the vice presidents and managers to whom they talk. A called-in management consultant usually settles only for the CEO's job.[43]

Whatever the reason, an outsider often seems to be able to accomplish something when an equally talented employee of the firm gets nowhere.

The other major question with respect to whom should perform operations audits is whether such audits should fall within the realm of the accountant. Historically, operations audits have been performed by internal auditors. Since internal auditors normally have an accounting background, the performance of operations audits have become associated with the accounting profession. Additionally, the term "audit" has an accounting connotation to it, which fact has caused some individuals who had little knowledge of operations auditing other than its benefits to call in an accountant when such an audit was desired. Most accounting firms with management services departments feel that operations audit engagements can eventually lead to a profitable management services engagement.

The performance of operations audits, however, does not necessarily require an accounting background. Some management consulting firms also undertake such engagements; however, most do not, since they feel that their real strength (and highest billings) is in problem solving, not problem locating.[44]

Some accountants accept such engagements only out of fear that someone else will accept the engagement and use the operations audit as a "foot-in-the-door" technique for obtaining the opportunity to perform the annual financial audit. It should also be noted that a partial operations audit is usually performed by the CPA firm in performing the financial audit. This "mini" operations audit culminates in the management letter that is (supposedly)[45] given to management annually at the completion of the audit.

Perhaps one of the definitions quoted earlier offers some explanation as to why accountants can perform operations audits equally as well, or better, than other professional groups:

The most important thing to appreciate is that there is no such thing as an operational audit. It is a question of approach and scope—the audit techniques are the same.[46]

Whatever the reasons, accountants (both internal and external) and management consultants do perform operations audits. The question of who performs such audits is not important. What is important is the increased interest in operations that results from an operations audit.

Summary

The role of the auditor has broadened in recent years. Management has become more aware that the bigness of businesses and the increasing strain on management time has caused a need for an outsider who will come in and give advice on various aspects of an organization. This need has been filled by operations auditors who will enter a department and identify problems. Operations auditing can actually be viewed as a control technique that provides management with a method for evaluating the effectiveness of operating procedures and various internal controls.

An operations audit is highly dependent upon questionnaires that are used in interviewing the personnel of the department or departments being audited. Through the results of these questionnaires and subsequent financial analyses, the auditor attempts to pinpoint problem areas. The auditor then communicates his findings to management. It is then up to management as to how the problem should be solved. The operations auditor does not solve the problem; his job is finished when the problem has been located and communicated to management.

3 Hospital Accounting and Auditing

For most industries the development of accounting procedures and auditing methodologies has been the role of the American Institute of Certified Public Accountants. Hospitals, however, have not followed this trend. The development of hospital accounting and auditing has been greatly influenced by the American Hospital Association, the Hospital Financial Management Association (formerly the American Association of Hospital Accountants), the Blue Cross plans, and government Medicare

The great majority of American hospitals belong to the American Hospital Assocation (AHA), which was founded in 1898. In 1918, a committee was formed to examine the problems of hospital accounting. That committee brought forth its first accounting manual in 1922. The overriding objective of the committee was the voluntary establishment of uniform accounting practices throughout the country.

The 1922 report recommended that hospitals segregate their accounts into two funds: the corporation accounts and the operating accounts.[1] The reason for separating accounts into two categories was to exclude from normal operations those types of expenses that varied from one hospital to another. The corporation accounts included land, buildings, equipment, endowment and trust funds, building funds, and investments. Also, the long-lived assets should include:

... an item of appreciation and depreciation, if in the judgment of the administrative board this should be considered in the corporation balance sheet.[2]

The expenses charged against the corporation accounts included interest expense, fund raising campaign expenses, and salaries of hospital officers.

The committee recommended that the operating accounts of hospitals provide for segregation of items by hospital function. This was particularly emphasized for expense accounts:

The departmentalization of operating expenses, it is believed, is a fundamental of proper hospital accounting and just as basic in arriving at the cost of the procedure as is the departmentalization of the expenses of operating various departments of an industry. If one attempts to combine the activities of the dietary, the nursing and the mechanical departments, their performance cannot be studied with the degree of efficiency that is possible if a definite chart of accounts by departments is set up and the cost of all commodities charged to the proper department. Specific reference is made to the practice in a large number of hospitals of carrying an item of "payroll" on their books in which account all salaries and wages of the hospital are charged. This does not permit proper control of funds.[3]

The 1922 committee also saw fit to remind hospital administrators that just having a good accounting system was not enough. The financial statements had to be analyzed regularly in order to be of any value:

Any recording system, whether it concerns professional, financial or administrative activity, is not productive nor does it approach its potentiality for good unless it furnishes a basis for the analysis of results. It is our belief that too much stress cannot be placed upon the necessity of having a routine mechanism for this purpose. Unless by arrangement an analysis of hospital records is made routinely, the tendency to neglect this very important phase of administrative duty under pressure of other work, is very great.[4]

It was recognized that country-wide uniformity of accounting principles would be a valuable step in measuring the efficiency of hospital management. At the time the committee report was issued, there were no comparisons that could be made between hospitals since there was no uniformity in any of the calculations.

Other recommendations of the 1922 report included that of hiring only highly qualified individuals to work in the accounting department. It was stated that accounting was no longer a process of recording historical events. Instead, accountants had to prepare up-to-date statistics that could be used in planning the day-to-day operations of the hospital. Another suggestion offered by the committee was that monthly financial statements should be prepared by the accounting department:

... the practice of some hospitals of waiting for the certified accountant at three, six and twelve month periods to furnish them with a statement of their financial performance sets up a handicap to administrative officers that is unfair. The accounting personnel of the institution should be competent to furnish figures to the administrative office immediately following the end of each month.[5]

Not many changes in hospital accounting resulted from the 1922 recommendations, particularly in regard to the usefulness of accounting information for the day-to-day operation of the hospital. One 1930 article authored by a leader in the area of hospital accounting noted that:

... there is a feeling at present among hospital administrators which is not unlike that expressed by managers of industrial enterprises 30 years ago, namely that a cost accounting system is a luxury and a nuisance, rather than a tool of control.[6]

The article also noted that there was little value in trying to compare hospitals by such ratios as cost per patient day since there was no uniform definition of what constituted an element of cost. Some hospitals included depreciation and other overhead costs, while other hospitals did not include such factors. In addition, there was not even agreement as to what constituted a patient. Some institutions included newborn infants; others did not. Variations in counting inpatients and outpatients was another problem.

The 1933 Committee Report

The major turning point in the development of hospital accounting came with the creation in 1933 of the American Hospital Association Advisory Committee on Accounting. From its inception, each member of the committee had an idea as to the ideal classification of accounts. Some of the ideas were based on uniform charts of accounts that had been developed for use by city- or state-regulated hospitals, and the major function of the committee chairman proved to be that of reconciling differences among committee members. Apparently, hospital financial managers had reached a stage where the worth of uniform financial data became realized. The problem facing the committee was the determination of exactly what constituted uniformity.

The published report emanating from the 1933 committee made four major specific recommendations relating to hospital accounting. The first recommendation was that balance sheets should be prepared regularly.[7] Prior to 1933, many hospitals never prepared a balance sheet despite their owning several million dollars worth of assets. It was recommended that the balance sheet consist of three types of funds: current, investments, and plant. Most hospitals kept adequate records of their current activities and investments, but the plant assets were often ignored altogether. This was attributable to the fact that plant assets were usually replaced by contributions or taxation, not the patient revenues of the hospitals. Since the assets were not expected to be replaced from money collected from patients, it was felt that there was no need to show the cost of such facilities as hospital expenses or as assets.

The second recommendation of the committee dealt with the classification of revenue.[8] Specifically, the idea was brought forth that revenues from patients should be categorized separately from income generated from the general community in the form of taxes or contributions. Allowances (charity cases, bad debts, and other adjustments) were to be deducted from gross revenues to arrive at the net revenues.

The third major recommendation (and perhaps the most important) was that hospitals should recognize such fixed charges as depreciation in statements of income and expense.[9] Many hospitals did not deduct depreciation expense since the fixed assets had been initially donated and it was assumed that replacements would be made available from future contributors. Therefore, there was no need to provide for depreciation from amounts collected from patients. Alternatively, there were some hospitals that did charge prices high enough to allow for future replacement of fixed assets, and these hospitals did deduct depreciation expense. Consequently, there was no uniformity in financial statements or statistical figures. The 1933 committee solved the problem by recommending "unanimously that interest and depreciation, as well as taxes and rent, be placed in a separate category to be designated as non-operating expense."[10]

This provision makes it possible for hospitals to compare costs in different institutions and for different periods of time. The basis of comparison may be merely the operating expenses, or the total expenses, including the fixed charges. In those cases where hospitals do not include allowances for depreciation the comparisons of operating costs will be legitimate; in those cases where hospitals include allowances for depreciation an examination of the records will reveal whether the allowances are reasonable estimates.[11]

The fourth idea brought forth by the 1933 committee was that hospital service is a group of joint products and that periodic cost analysis should be made for each of the various types of service.[12] Although the third feature of the committee report, the recognition of depreciation expense, is the most important feature for external reporting purposes, it is this fourth recommendation that is most important for internal reporting purposes. The idea of periodic cost analysis by type of service was to provide hospital administrators with the opportunity to compare and improve managerial efficiency in a manner similar to that in manufacturing industries.

During the two decades following the issuance of the 1933 committee report, there were few innovations in accounting for hospitals. Many hospitals implemented the recommendations of the 1933 committee, at least in regard to the preparation of financial statements and the preparation of periodic cost analyses. The recording of depreciation expense, however, was slow to be accepted as the following excerpt from a 1954 article indicates:

The lack of necessity of accounting for profit and of keeping records for tax purposes, combined with the fact that hospital buildings are usually purchased and constructed with specially collected building fund donations, result in many instances in lack of accurate accounting for the value of plant and equipment. Matters are further complicated by the fact that depreciation accounting is not yet recognized as necessary, or even as reasonable, for philanthropic institutions.[13]

The publication in 1950 of *Uniform Hospital Statistics and Classification of Accounts* by the AHA recommended that hospitals utilize fund accounting with four types of funds. The additional type of fund over that recommended in 1933 was a Temporary Fund.

The period from 1933 to 1954 did see the beginning of something that was to have a major impact on hospital financial management. During that era, there was a significant increase in the number of individuals covered by Blue Cross plans and other types of hospitalization insurance. In 1954, it was estimated that nearly 50 percent of hospital patients had their bills paid by one of these plans.[14]

During the early years, the amounts paid by the Blue Cross plans were rates established by the insurers. Although Blue Cross tried to match hospital costs, such was often difficult because of the variations among various hospitals:

> The substantial differences in rates between institutions indicated that the method of payment of stated charges would not meet their needs in the long run. Although it is not a panacea, cost reimbursement is in use by government agencies, Blue Cross insurance plans, and some commercial insurance companies. Under this principle they pay the health facility what it actually costs to provide patient services.[15]

Cost Reimbursement

During the late 1950s the Blue Cross plans began reimbursing hospitals on the basis of costs incurred. Cost reimbursement, having been used previously by various units of government, was not a new concept, but the increasing popularity of Blue Cross made cost reimbursement a topic that affected all hospitals to a great degree. Charging for patient care at cost (or cost plus a small percentage) necessitated improving their accounting methods in order to design procedures for gathering cost data.

With the coming of cost reimbursement plans came an increased acceptance of depreciation as a normal hospital expense. Since the Blue Cross plans would reimburse a hospital for depreciation expense, it was profitable for a hospital to deduct depreciation on its statement of revenues and expenses. One difference, however, between the depreciation expense of hospitals and other industries is that for hospitals, depreciation is an expense requiring a cash outlay.

> However, to be properly included as a cost under a cost reimbursement type contract, depreciation should be currently funded within each fiscal period; that is, cash in an amount equivalent to the total depreciation charge should be transferred from the General Fund to the plant, building or some other similar fund. Otherwise money received as reimbursement for depreciation expense could be used for other purposes, such as providing for the cost of free care to indigent patients. Then when the plant assets required replacing, the cash would not be available but would have to be obtained through contributions or other sources.[16]

As can be surmised from the above quotation, bad debt expense is not considered as a reimbursable cost. The argument is that bad debts do not arise from servicing the individual for whom the reimbursement is being made; therefore, it can not be considered in the computation of hospital costs for reimbursement purposes.

It is interesting to note the similarity of the development of depreciation accounting among hospitals to that of profit-oriented industries. Despite all of the theoretical arguments that depreciation should be recorded as an expense, such was not done with any uniformity or regularity until it became economically beneficial for the entity to show the deduction. For profit-making businesses, it was the corporate income tax law in 1909 that provided the financial incentive to record depreciation while the tax exempt hospital did not find it financially lucrative to do so until the cost reimbursement plans came into common usage.

The Health Insurance for the Aged Act (Medicare) was passed by Congress in 1965. The Act is administered by the Social Security Administration, but the seventy-six Blue Cross Associations in the various states act as agents between hospitals and the Social Security Administration.[17] This Act resulted in an improvement in cost finding and accounting procedures for those hospitals that had not implemented sound procedures for Blue Cross purposes.[18]

The most recent accounting recommendations from the American Hospital Association came in the 1966 publication *Chart of Accounts for Hospitals*. There was little change from previous AHA recommendations with two exceptions. The AHA preferred that long-term security investments be reported at current market values and that property, plant, and equipment be reported at current replacement costs.[19] Other assets are still to be carried at historical cost.

Hospital Auditing

The development of hospital auditing can be compared to the development of auditing in general, only a little more slowly. Auditing for fraud purposes continued much longer. Early audits of hospitals were performed by state auditors and committees of the board of trustees.[20] The lack of use of financial statements by outside investors contributed to the slow development of hospital auditing.

By the 1930s, other auditors occasionally came into contact with hospitals as the Blue Cross plans began utilizing auditors as did banks who lent money to hospitals. Still, auditing was performed primarily to determine whether money was being spent in a manner proscribed by state law or clauses in trust fund agreements.

The American Institute of Certified Public Accountants did not contribute much to the literature of hospital auditing until after World War II. Even then, the only contribution was a few articles in the *Journal of Accountancy*. The first major publication dealing with hospital auditing was Case Studies in Auditing Procedures Number 11, *A Hospital*, published in the summer of 1956. Other articles in the *Journal of Accountancy* followed.

The next major publications came only recently in the form of two audit guides, *Medicare Audit Guide* and *Hospital Audit Guide*. The latter of these is perhaps most significant in that, for the first time, it is recognized that hospital audits may be made for other than specialized or compliance purposes. The *Guide* emphasizes that hospital financial statements are "being used by credit grantors, government agencies, and the community."[21] As a result, hospital financial statements should be prepared in accordance with generally accepted accounting principles, which means that hospitals are subject to the requirements contained in Opinions of the Accounting Principles Board and Statements of the Financial Accounting Standards Board:

Recommendations in the revised American Hospital Association's *Chart of Accounts for Hospitals* (1966) are generally compatible with generally accepted accounting principles and this guide. However, two recommendations in that publication presently are not in accordance with generally accepted accounting principles:

1. Carrying property, plant, and equipment at current replacement cost and basing depreciation on these values.
2. Carrying long-term security investments at current market value.[22]

It is interesting to note that two of the members of the AICPA Committee on Health Care Institutions dissented to the requirement that investments must be carried at cost.

The passage of the Medicare Act has had an influence on the extent of hospital auditing. Blue Cross plans have always had the option of auditing hospital records, but such audits are now formalized for Medicare purposes. The intermediary may utilize its own auditors or may contract out audits to independent public accounting firms. In addition, the Medicare Act provides that hospital records may also be audited by the General Accounting Office, the Department of Health, Education and Welfare, and the Social Security Administration. The purposes of these audits are as follows:

1. To ascertain that the hospital is conforming to the Health Insurance Act for the Aged with respect to the payments thereunder.
2. To review, analyze, test, and verify the hospital's financial and statistical books and records and to determine that only proper items of cost applicable to hospital services have been included in reimbursable cost.
3. To verify on a selective basis that expenses attributable to the health insurance program have been reasonably determined.
4. To ascertain that records supporting statistical data and the adequacy of the methods used for accumulation are sufficient to properly develop valid and accurate statistical information.
5. To make maximum utilization of hospital audits performed by others, where applicable, insofar as they reasonably further the audit objectives of the Bureau of Health Insurance.[23]

In addition to annual financial audits by independent CPAs and audits by health insurers (both private and federal), some hospitals are also subject to audit by state audit agencies.[24]

Operations Auditing

In spite of the fact that hospitals are subject to numerous financial and compliance audits, it seems readily apparent that another type of audit could be advantageous. An operations audit to appraise the problems of hospital policies and practices would seem especially appropriate. Private businesses utilize the technique of operations auditing to judge managerial effectiveness and to isolate problem areas of the firm. Hospitals could also benefit from the technique. In fact, nonprofit hospitals might be more appropriately suited for operations audits than firms that are organized with profitable intent.

The lack of the profit motive and the requirement that a nonprofit hospital serve charity cases makes the examination of financial statements a poor method of judging hospital management. For this reason, it is necessary to observe the actual operations of each department in order to determine whether or not that department has operating problems.

Unlike other industries, large hospitals did not follow the trend of converting internal auditors to operations auditors.[25] and small hospitals do not have internal auditors at all. As a result, few hospitals have ever been subject to a true operations audit. Those hospitals that have had operations audits normally hired an outside accounting or management consulting firm to perform the audit.[26] These audits were usually for a single department or functional area and were often necessitated by a major problem of some type.

The American Hospital Association has even recommended something similar to an operations audit in its Management Review Program. The AHA Management Review Program is a technique for self-evaluation in certain functional areas such as governing authority, nursing service, emergency department, dietary, housekeeping, and laundry.[27] A hospital with an up-to-date internal auditing staff could expand the review program into a full-scale operations audit.

Since large hospitals have not transformed their internal auditors into operations auditors, and small hospitals do not have internal auditors (or operations auditors), the only alternative is for hospitals to hire outside auditors to come in and perform operations audits.

Operations auditing of hospitals seems to offer opportunities to both the auditor and the auditee. CPA firms can increase their audit and management services business, while hospitals can reduce the number of operating problems and hopefully reduce the cost of health care.

Summary

Hospital accounting has been influenced primarily by the American Hospital Association, the Hospital Financial Management Association, the Blue Cross plans, and Medicare. Hospital auditing has been most influenced by the Blue

Cross plans, Medicare and, most recently, by the American Institute of Certified Public Accountants.

Hospital audits have traditionally been for compliance purposes as state and federal agencies and other third-party payers required an independent observer to check cost computations and uses of funds. More recently, hospitals have begun publishing audited annual reports for financial purposes much in the same manner as businesses operated for profit. Due to their small size, the majority of hospitals do not have internal auditing departments. Consequently, operations audits of hospitals have been almost nonexistent. Perhaps the lack of a profit incentive and the opportunity to pass costs on to third-party payers have been contributing factors to the lack of operations audits.

When applied to nonprofit hospitals, the benefits of operations audits should accrue to the public at large through lower hospital charges and health insurance rates. Therefore, it is concluded that hospitals should utilize operations auditing in order to isolate problems for possible solution.

The next two chapters outline and describe an audit program complete with questionnaires that can be used in performing an operations audit for six key hospital departments.

4

Development of an Operations Audit Model

The Need for a Model

An operations audit of a hospital is a large undertaking. A hospital is an integrated business consisting of hundreds of functions performed by hundreds of employees. Such is the vastness of the hospital operation that very few employee job descriptions are identical to those of other employees. In order to perform an operations audit at a hospital, even a small hospital, it is essential that a framework exist by which the auditor can be guided in his work. A model, combined with a detailed audit program, would provide the groundwork necessary for an operations audit to be performed.

Although operations audits have been performed for years by the General Accounting Office and numerous private firms, there has never been a comprehensive model developed that could be generalized to fit any operations audit. This is perhaps attributable to the fact that most operations audits are performed by internal auditors within a single entity and when multiple entities (or divisions within an entity) are involved, there is sufficient difference among the organizations to alleviate the possibility of generalizing most parts of the audit. Secondly, the lack of an operations audit model may be attributable to a lack of interest on the topic by academicians and researchers. This lack of interest is partially evidenced by the fact that no major auditing textbook offers more than a couple of paragraphs on the topic and no university in the Southeast offers a course on the topic.[1]

As discussed in Chapters 1 and 3, hospitals are particularly well suited to the use of operations audits because of the broad nature of the activities performed. Additionally, an operations audit model would be beneficial in the performance of such audits. Furthermore, a generalized operations audit model for hospitals is quite feasible since the similarity of operations among various hospitals warrants the expenditures of the time and research necessary to prepare such a model. The model can then serve as the framework for operations audits at numerous hospitals and thus result in time savings to future auditors who can make use of the generalized model and corresponding audit questionnaires.

An audit model is not a new idea. Mautz and Sharaf in their study, *The Philosophy of Auditing*, developed a generalized model for a financial audit. This chapter begins where Mautz and Sharaf stopped by developing a comprehensive operations audit model for a small hospital. Although there have been many journal articles on the topic of operations auditing, most have been of the definitive type. The most all-inclusive work, *Operations Auditing* by Lindberg and Cohn, discusses the topic from the point of view of an internal auditor working in a manufacturing firm. The two-stage aspect of the audit (preliminary and in-depth) advocated in these earlier works is assumed for purposes of this research. This chapter is primarily concerned with the preliminary stage while Chapter 5 deals with the in-depth portion of the audit.

Preliminary Steps

There are four basic steps that comprise the preliminary stage of the audit. These are (1) a physical walking tour of the facility, (2) acquisition of written data, (3) interviews with management personnel, and (4) certain financial analysis work. The results of these four steps are summarized in a preliminary audit report that is commonly called a survey memorandum. This survey memorandum is not given to anyone; it is merely used by the auditor to determine which departments will require an in-depth audit. An in-depth examination is only performed for those departments where it appears most likely that serious problems exist and material benefit could result from their solution.

Physical Tour

Direct observation can often be the most productive source of information about an entity or one of its subdivisions. Therefore, the operations auditor must conduct a physical tour of the facilities being audited:

> The auditor who consciously observes will become aware of many problems that are not recorded or are incapable of analysis through data. Feelings of openness, communication freedom, respect for subordinates, manner in which supervision is performed, neatness, housekeeping, and so forth tell a good deal about conditions in the unit being audited. Observation is also a rich source of specific examples that are useful in illustrating general conclusions.[2]

Another author explained the physical walk-through as follows:

> Every operations audit includes a survey of physical facilities. One of the purposes of this survey is the identification of areas which appear to merit special attention—the approach follows the "management by exception" philosophy.... During this tour the auditor could observe conditions which—perhaps because of their very obviousness—may have escaped the attention of local management.[3]

Thus, the criteria and objectives are the same in the physical tour stage as in the interview with management stage; in effect, the auditor could take the questionnaire he later uses when interviewing management and ask himself the same questions.

In the physical tour stage of the operations audit and in the other stages of the audit as well, the auditor is searching for indications of problems. For example, during a physical walk-through of an operation (whether hospital or otherwise), a discovery might be made of the existence of idle equipment, which would indicate that the entity is not earning the maximum return on its investment. In addition, touring the hospital business offices provides the auditor with the opportunity to view the entire operation and obtain an overall general impression of the organization.

Normally, the auditor will be accompanied on the physical tour by either the hospital administrator or the controller. Either prior to, or simultaneous with, the physical tour, the auditor should discuss with the tour director the reason for the audit to determine whether it was prompted by a specific problem or merely as preventive therapy.[4] The administrator or controller should acquaint employees with the reasons for the audit and the benefits that are expected. Employees should be made to understand that the audit is not an implied criticism of their efforts, but an effort to make them more effective in their work.[5]

The auditor must keep in mind at all times that the purpose of the physical tour is basically to orient the auditor to the institution being audited. However, the physical tour is an integral part of the preliminary stage of the audit, and the overall purpose of the preliminary stage is to select departments for further audit during the in-depth portion of the audit. The physical tour, though often called an orientation tour, is not just for orientation to the hospital, but is also oriented toward the discovery of potential problems.

At the end of this section (see p. 00) is the list of questions that an operations auditor should ask himself as he proceeds through the physical tour of a hospital. These questions have been selected from the departmental questionnaires that are shown in Appendixes A through F and are described fully in the next chapter. All of the auditor's questions can be answered by observation without explanation from the administrator or controller. The questions have been categorized by department when specific questions apply only to certain departments. Otherwise, the questions are normally applicable to all departments and are so listed.

It must be pointed out that no aspect of the preliminary stage of the audit should be considered as positive proof of the existence of problems. The auditor's questions have been designed so that a "no" answer indicates a possible problem. This should be considered as prima facie evidence only, however, since such a small amount of time is spent in each department during the physical tour. Even though the results of the physical tour may give strong indication that a particular department is having problems, further audit steps may indicate otherwise. The objective of the preliminary stage is to make several, rather quick analyses and hopefully pinpoint one or more departments that have more problems than the others. The physical tour serves not only to orient the auditor to all of the departments under consideration, but also aids the auditor in selecting departments that need in-depth study.

Some questions will always be easily answered as a result of the tour. For instance, questions 26 (Is there a centralized personnel function . . . ?), 27 (Is personnel a separate department from payroll?), 38 (Is there a centralized receiving function?), and 43 (Are the storerooms conveniently close to the receiving dock?) will always be answered during the physical tour. If these questions are not answered, then the tour was incomplete and should be rescheduled.

It is the opinion of this writer that the list of auditor's questions should not be carried along on the physical tour, but instead should be answered from memory after the tour. This, however, does not mean that the auditor should not take notes during the tour if there are sufficient unusual situations that the auditor might tend to forget some of them. Some operations auditors have even recommended that the auditor carry a camera during the tour and snap pictures of areas that need drastic improvement.[6] The pictures would not only serve to refresh the auditor's memory at a later time, but might also provide material that could be used in the final audit report.

The physical tour is the stage of the audit where the auditor can best make use of his inventiveness. The tour can be used not only as orientation for future use, but also for initial discoveries of both good and bad situations. The auditor must use the list of questions as a guideline, but it should not be used as the total source of information resulting from the physical tour. The benefits to the auditor (and subsequently the hospital) resulting from the physical tour will be correlated to the auditor's initiative and ability to observe the "forest beyond the trees."

The following is a list of the auditor's physical tour questions:

All Departments:
1. Are the physical facilities of the department adequate?
2. Is there an adequate amount of office equipment available in the department?
3. Are machines and equipment being used to maximum capacity?
4. Does there appear to be an excessive amount of equipment in the department?
5. Does office layout lend itself to the normal flow of operations?
6. Are physical conditions (smell, heat, etc.) of the department satisfactory?
7. Is lighting adequate?
8. Does the proper amount of floor space exist in the department?
9. Are aisles and doorways wide enough for traffic?
10. Is storage space adequate?

11. Is the department overstocked with supplies that it will either not use in the near future or will never use?
12. Is there an adequate supply of fire extinguishers?
13. Does the hospital have a suggestion box?
14. Is all filing of records kept up to date?
15. Is copying machine use controlled?
16. Is a record kept of reasons for long distance calls?
17. Is the departmental staff large enough?
18. Are employees in view of supervision?
19. Are all tasks that are performed necessary?

Accounting and Payroll Departments:
20. Are employee time cards used?
21. Does anyone oversee the clocking-in process?
22. Are checks kept locked up when not being used?
23. Is a check protector used?

Patient Census Management Department:
24. Does each admitting and discharge officer have a private office?
25. Has the feasibility of accepting charge cards (Master Charge, Bank Americard) been examined?

Personnel Department:
26. Is there a centralized personnel function through which all applicants must pass?
27. Is personnel a separate department from payroll?
28. Is a nondiscrimination policy clearly stated and posted?
29. Does the personnel department maintain an open door policy to all employees?
30. Do interviewers have their own private offices?
31. Is the department easy to reach by the public?
32. Is the department easy to reach by employees?
33. Is there a bulletin board available for communication of information to hospital employees?
34. Is there an internal newspaper or magazine for hospital employees?

Purchasing Department:
35. Are quantities purchased consistent with actual requirements?
36. Do purchase orders normally include prices?
37. Is there an adequate library of catalogs and current price lists?

Receiving and Materials Handling Department:
38. Is there a centralized receiving function?

39. Do all goods that are received come through the receiving department?
40. Is the department kept in neat order?
41. Are all materials easily accessible when needed?
42. Are all items counted as they are unloaded?
43. Are the storerooms conveniently close to the receiving dock?
44. Is access to storeroom restricted to specific employees?
45. Are packages date-stamped upon receipt in order to determine time lapse between receipt and delivery to the user?

Acquisition of Written Data

The objective of the operations auditor is to determine whether or not an operation enjoys consistent management practices. Consequently, it is imperative that the auditor obtain documentation with which departmental data can be compared. Types of written documentation that the auditor should acquire would include the following:

1. Written Goals and Objectives;
2. Policies and Procedures Manuals;
3. Job Descriptions;
4. Organization Charts;
5. Budgets;
6. Internal Departmental Reports;
7. Financial Statements;
8. HAS Reports (Hospital Advisory Services);
9. Flow Charts;
10. Forms Used;
11. Minutes of the Board of Directors Meetings.

It is usually possible to obtain much of the above data during the physical tour stage of the audit or the interviews with management stage. Therefore, the acquisition of written data is not necessarily a separate stage in performing the audit; it can actually be incorporated with the other stages. However, it should be considered as a separate stage by the auditor for planning purposes.

The objective of the acquisition of data stage of the audit is different than that of the other stages in that the auditor is not necessarily trying to arrive at a conclusion. Instead, the auditor's major emphasis is to obtain raw material for future stages of the audit. This is not to say that the auditor will never obtain important information directly from the data acquisition stage. For example, if some of the documents were not readily available, or never existed, the auditor would perhaps conclude that the lack of such documentation was an indication of a problem situation.

It must be remembered that the operations auditor has two sources for standards of measurement. These sources are the individual hospital and the industry. For the discovery of individual hospital standards the auditor must rely on the data accumulated during this stage of the audit. Particularly important to the auditor in the learning of hospital standards are goals, objectives, policies, and procedures.

Written goals and objectives are important for both the hospital as a whole and for the individual departments. Without goals and objectives that are known to all employees, there is danger that various departments will not all be oriented toward the same final objectives. Written goals and objectives help insure that there is unity, continuity, and consistency in a hospital.[7] The auditor must also assure himself that there has been more activity than just setting goals and objectives. Goals and objectives must be communicated to all individuals in the organization.

There should also be a periodic follow-up to determine whether established goals and objectives are being met. Not only can goals and objectives lead all elements of an organization to the same conclusion, but they can also serve as a means of evaluating segments of the organization.

Policies and procedures manuals can help to insure adherence to stated goals and objectives. Such manuals can serve as a reference source when no precedent for a particular action exists. Consequently, all employees would tend to react similarly in a given situation and thus consistency of action is the result. The auditor will want to ascertain whether written policies and procedures are being properly carried out. If not, the organization is either acting incorrectly or the manual should be changed to reflect the change to the new procedure.

Written *job descriptions* permit management and the operations auditor to effectively determine whether or not a given employee is meeting the obligations of his job. Without job descriptions the employee could always rationalize a less than adequate performance with the statement "that's not my job." Job descriptions are also valuable when a position is being filled with a new employee. A written job description would give the personnel director a guideline that could be used in measuring the qualifications of applicants.

A well-communicated *organization chart* should be available. An employee should know where he stands in relation to other employees:

An organization chart ... serves as an authoritative source of information. Official answers to organization questions are provided. Allocation of activities by specific positions is direct and clear cut. Disputes involving jurisdiction over activities can be settled, and information as to who handles a specific task can be readily ascertained.[8]

As was pointed out in Chapter 1, hospital organization charts are quite complicated and the written charts are often erroneous. The auditor will want to determine whether the written organization chart is identical to the de facto organization chart.

Written *budgets* are prepared a year in advance for most hospitals. The auditor should obtain a copy of the master budget for use in the subsequent financial analysis stage of the audit. In addition, the auditor will want to assure himself that the budget is used and not merely prepared. The budget should be both a planning tool and a control tool.

All examples of *internal departmental reports* should be obtained by the auditor. Some of the reports will prove valuable for financial analysis work. Other reports should be examined for necessity and overlap. There is little point, for instance, in continuing to prepare reports that were required for defense purposes during World War II.

Both interim and annual *financial statements* should be obtained by the auditor for use in performing financial analysis work. Prior years' statements should also be acquired since they would be necessary in order to do any trend analysis.

Hospital Advisory Services (HAS) Reports, if available, should be obtained by the auditor for use in the financial analysis stage of the audit. The HAS reports are departmentalized financial ratios that are prepared for the individual hospital, the state average, and the national average. They are published by the American Hospital Association. All information for the state and national averages are categorized by bed size.[9] Over 90 percent of the hospitals in North Carolina and South Carolina subscribe and contribute to HAS. This percentage is considerably lower nationally.[10]

Flow charts, when available, can help employees of the hospital and the operations auditor better understand how an operation is supposed to be run. If written flow charts are not available, the auditor may sketch his own for purposes of understanding a particular problem.

The auditor will want to obtain copies of *all forms that are used by the departments under study*. This will enable the auditor to determine such things as whether the size of the forms is appropriate for easy filing and whether spacing on the form is correct for easy typing. The auditor may also observe whether several departments might be able to utilize the same form if certain changes were to be made. The necessity of information recorded on the forms is another factor the auditor should include in the examination.

Finally, *minutes of the board of directors meetings* are often useful in further orienting the auditor as to hospital goals and objectives and indicating whether or not there is agreement on all phases of goals and objectives. Particular problem situations might also be uncovered much more easily than might be the case if the minutes were not read.

As with the physical tour, the auditor should not consider the above list of written data as all inclusive. If anything else is observed or offered, the auditor should obtain copies.

Interviews with Management

Operations auditing relies on what people perceive and feel as much as it does on recorded data and statistics. The operations auditor learns from people. Consequently, interviews with individual managers are an integral part of the preliminary phase of the operations audit. The experts in a particular hospital are the people that run the hospital. Therefore, the auditor can obtain his best information by asking hospital managers what the problems are. Naturally, this is not as easy as it sounds. It is up to the auditor to ferret out the problem situations by asking the proper questions. Often a manager is not aware that a problem exists because the immediate problems of day-to-day work have caused the overall hospital objectives to be subjugated to the problem of keeping the top of a desk clear of papers. In other situations, as explained in Chapter 2, individual managers may be aware of problems but cannot convince top management that such a problem exists.

The departmental questionnaires (shown in Appendixes A through F) are for use in determining the *level* of management's problems within various departments during the in-depth stage of a hospital operations audit. The same questions usually will not be used when interviewing management during the preliminary stage of the audit since the auditor's objectives are not the same as they will be during the in-depth stage. For that reason, the preliminary-stage management questions listed at the end of this section (see p. 00) were compiled. These questions were selected from the departmental questionnaires with the criteria for selection being the importance rating given the question by hospital department heads. (See the appendix section for the importance rating assigned to each question; the criteria for inclusion in the list of management questions was an importance rating at least 1.5 standard deviations above the mean score of all questions on each departmental questionnaire in the appendix section.)

For convenience, the list of preliminary-stage management questions has been categorized by department. This categorization has no significance during the interview; it is only for the auditor's benefit when the responses are analyzed. All of the questions should be asked of all managers including those who have, or should have, some knowledge of departments besides their own. Normally, among this group would be the following persons:

1. Administrator;
2. Controller;
3. Admitting and Discharge Supervisor;
4. Payroll Supervisor;
5. Accounting Supervisor;

6. Purchasing Agent;
7. Receiving Supervisor;
8. Personnel Director.

The same questions should be asked in interviewing each respondent. It might seem that to ask several individuals the same questions would be redundant but as others have pointed out:

This is not a wasteful suggestion because "facts" are seldom presented in the same way or equally emphasized by all the people who observe them. The objective truth—which is inherently difficult to find—is more likely to be unearthed if the auditor obtains multiple answers to the same question.[11]

Overall, the operations auditor should be constantly alert for problem situations that do not show themselves as a result of the use of the questions; they should never become a crutch to the auditor or cause the auditor to restrict his judgment.

The following is a list of the preliminary-stage management questions:

Personnel Department:
1. Is there an up-to-date published statement of personnel policies and procedures available to all hospital employees?
2. Is there an established wage and salary program to insure equitable rates of pay?
3. Are accurate and complete personnel records kept for each employee?
4. Is there a system for immediate notification of the personnel department when an employee is terminated?
5. Do you feel that personnel employees are knowledgeable about personnel policies and employee benefits?
6. Do you feel that hospital employees understand the personnel policies?
7. Does the personnel department have an open line of communication with all department heads and managers?

Payroll Department:
8. Is an employee's initial salary authorized in writing by someone qualified to do so?
9. Are salary changes authorized in writing?
10. Are employees paid by check?
11. Is payroll always completed on time?
12. Are time cards kept long enough to meet legal requirements?
13. Are quarterly tax reports always filed on time?
14. Are withholding tax deposits always made on time?
15. How often are errors made in the preparation of payroll?

Purchasing Department:
16. Does the hospital utilize a centralized purchasing system?
17. Is there an inventory control system?
18. Does the purchasing department have good relations with other departments?
19. Does the purchasing department try to buy products that meet the needs of several departments rather than stocking several brands of nearly identical items?

Receiving Department:
20. Is there a centralized receiving function?
21. Do all goods that are received come through the receiving department?
22. Does the receiving department check shipments for damages?
23. Are items which are radioactive, perishable, or require controlled temperatures always delivered immediately to the user?
24. Is there an adequate supply of fire extinguishers?

Patient Census Management Department:
25. Have formal admissions policies and procedures been developed?
26. Have formal discharge policies and procedures been developed?
27. Does the hospital have a written financial policy to give or tell patients?
28. Are admissions and discharge personnel knowledgeable enough to read and understand insurance policies?

Accounting Department:
29. Does the accounting department provide pertinent historical and projected financial data accurately, speedily, and in meaningful form?
30. Is it hospital policy to have receipts deposited in the bank and recorded in the cash receipts journal daily?
31. Is the bank statement reconciled monthly?
32. Are financial statements and internal reports prepared monthly?
33. Are all revenues and expenses always posted to the proper department?
34. Do all charges get posted promptly to the proper patient accounts?
35. Are statements mailed out regularly to former patients who still owe a portion of their bill?

All Departments:
36. Are problems that affect work discussed with the head nurses or other department heads of the area that is at fault?
37. Are the employees in your department and the other departments with which you are familiar well qualified to perform the duties that are required of them?

38. Do you feel that all employees within your department, and the other departments with which you are familiar, keep the information that they come in contact with confidential?
39. Is there an open line of communication between your department and the individuals to whom you report?
40. Do you feel that all departments treat patients with warmth and courtesy?
41. Do all of the forms that you come in contact with have spaces for all needed information?
42. Is lighting adequate in all offices?
43. Are sufficient machines and equipment available to those who need them?
44. Is the communication between your department and other departments satisfactory?
45. Do you feel that you are provided with all information you need to fulfill your responsibilities?
46. Do you feel that all sections of the hospital business office have a good public relations image?
47. Are job descriptions available for each position?
48. Do you feel that everyone in your department has a thorough understanding of their job?

Financial Analysis Work

The final segment of the preliminary audit is the financial analysis work performed by the auditor. The data accumulation stage of the audit should be instrumental in obtaining the documentation necessary for financial analysis work.

If the hospital being audited subscribes to HAS (Hospital Advisory Services) Reports, the financial analysis work of the auditor is greatly simplified since several ratios are already computed that will be of interest to the auditor. Not only do the HAS Reports provide current data on the hospital, the state averages, and the national averages, by bed size, but they also compare the hospital's data against the current year's budget. Thus, it is easy for the auditor to "eyeball" the reports and spot exceptional variances. (See Appendix H for a sample HAS Report illustrating the national averages of hospitals with from 100 to 149 beds; the figures are categorized into nine regions based upon geographic location.)

Numerous items included in HAS Reports are valuable to the operations auditor undertaking an assignment in a hospital business office. Such items as can be taken from the Reports are categorized in the following list by the departments for which the ratios or percentages would be applicable:

Patient Census Management Department:
1. Full-Time Employee per Occupied Bed
2. Full-Time Employee per Bed
3. Days of Revenue in Patient Accounts Receivable
4. Medical + Surgical Units % Occupancy
5. Average Length of Stay—Medical and Surgical
6. Operating Room Visits per 100 Medical + Surgical Admissions
7. Reserve as a % of Accounts Receivable

Purchasing, Personnel, Accounting, and Payroll Departments:
1. Administration + Fiscal Services—Expense Percentage
2. Administration Manhours per Bed
3. Fiscal Services Manhours per Bed
4. Deductions From Patient Revenue

Receiving and Materials Handling Department:
1. Central Services Expense Percentage
2. Line Items per Manhour
3. Line Items per Patient Day
4. Central Services and Supply Revenue Percentage

The number of full-time employees per bed and per occupied bed could be an indicator of overall hospital efficiency since the indication might be that there are too many or too few employees for a particular sized hospital. Conversely (and the reason the ratio is categorized under patient management), a high number of employees per occupied bed might be an indication that not enough beds are occupied. That could be attributable to a lack of demand for hospital services or to inefficiency in the area of patient census management. In some hospitals, the only reason beds are empty is because no one knows that they are empty.[1,2]

The percentage of occupancy in the medical and surgical units is also an indicator of a possible breakdown in communication with the people who are supposed to keep the beds filled. Comparison with the budgeted figures is as equally important as comparison with state and national averages since new hospitals are often built with excess capacity to allow for future growth. Therefore, if the auditor is auditing a hospital with excess capacity, the averages for other hospitals may be meaningless. The excess capacity, however, should have been considered when the current year's budget was prepared.

The average length of stay statistic for medical and surgical patients may help to explain an unusual variance in the above percentage of occupancy figure. If the average length of stay appears unusual, it may be attributable to inefficient scheduling of admissions or excesive (unneeded) pressure on doctors to discharge patients early.

The percentage of operating room visits to medical and surgical admissions is an indicator of the efficiency of patient mix. A hospital cannot survive if it is operating only as a rest home. A hospital must sell drugs, perform operations, give blood tests, physical therapy, and perform numerous other activities in order to break even. The daily room rent does not permit a hospital to cover its costs. It must sell other services besides a bed and a meal. It is the responsibility of the admissions department to schedule patients, when possible, so that there is a broad range of services required.[13] The more complicated and severe the medical problem, the more profit there is for the hospital. If only a small percentage of patients visit the operating room during a period of time, it may be because the admissions department is giving preferential treatment to less severe illnesses.

The final statistic categorized under patient census management is the number of days of revenue in patient accounts receivable. An extremely high or low figure, as compared to the averages, could indicate unusual activity in either the area of patient census management or accounting. It is the responsibility of the admission clerks to determine the manner of payment prior to admitting a patient. If there are no third-party payers, the admissions clerk should try and obtain payment in advance. Discharge clerks should try and collect any monies that are not paid before discharging a patient. Since the area of patient census management has two opportunities to collect from patients, an effective department can reduce receivables. If the patient is not able to pay before being discharged, then payment arrangements are made. It then becomes the responsibility of the accounting department to collect the money. If the accounting department fails to send out statements or does not pressure the debtors for payment, then receivables will mount upward. If the number of days of revenue included in receivables is high, the operations auditor will need further data in order to determine which of the two departments might be at fault. Internal reports prepared by the patient census management staff are often available that will shed additional light on the collection situation.[14]

The statistics that relate to accounting, payroll, purchasing, and personnel include the administrative and fiscal services expense percentage. The auditor will only be able to get a general idea of a good or bad situation since all four departments are included in the one figure.

Administration manhours per bed could be more meaningful since that figure relates to purchasing and personnel (plus the hospital administrator and chaplaincy service). An unusually high or low number of hours per bed could indicate that purchasing and personnel were over or understaffed.

Fiscal services manhours per bed relate to accounting and payroll and could be an indicator of staffing problems in those departments.

The reserve as a percentage of accounts receivable statistic (if high) could indicate a lack of aggressiveness by the accounting department in collecting past due accounts. Again, comparison with prior periods and similar sized hospitals in the state provide meaningful standards that can be employed by the operations auditor.

The last of the accounting department statistics, deductions from patient revenue, expresses the percentage that certain deductions are of revenue. The deductions relate to special discounts to certain classes of patients such as welfare cases and the clergy. An abnormally high figure for this statistic could be indicative of an over liberal policy, or perhaps of employee fraud.

There are four statistics that can be utilized by the operations auditor in searching for problems in the area of receiving and materials handling. An abnormally large unfavorable variance in the central services expense percentage might be caused by either operating problems or employee theft. If the central services and supply revenue percentage is also abnormally high, the possibility of theft may be ruled out. If both figures are high, then there is an indication of problems, but at least the excessive costs are being passed along to the patient and the hospital is not losing. If the revenue percentage is unusually low, then there is support for the belief that all costs are not being passed along to the patient. Perhaps the billing system is at fault.

The two statistics, line items per manhour and line items per patient day, relate to the number of requisitions processed. A line item is a description on a requisition form and has no relationship to the quantity of items requisitioned. An unusually high figure per manhour might be indicative that too many requisitions are being processed and steps should be taken to have departments send out requisitions less frequently. An unusually low number of line items per manhour might be indicative of too few requests. Departments may be storing large quantities of supplies rather than requesting items more frequently. As a result, excessive inventories may have to be carried. Since supplies should constitute a variable cost, the statistic line items per patient day enables the auditor to assess the problem situations of the materials handling workers from still another viewpoint.

Survey Memorandum

The auditor should now be prepared to organize all of the data and recommend one or more departments for further study. In effect, the auditor prepares an audit report covering the findings made during the preliminary stage of the operations audit. However, this audit report is never seen by anyone other than the operations auditor. The purpose of preparing a survey memorandum is to force the auditor to organize his findings and thoughts. The operations auditor has made a physical walk-through of the hospital, has talked to numerous department heads concerning their beliefs, and obtained numerous internal documents. The sheer quantity of the data obtained would exceed the auditor's ability to comprehend the situation if there were not a systematic organization of the findings resulting from the preliminary audit.

The survey memorandum (refer to Appendix G for an illustration) is the document that the auditor uses to help decide what department will be selected for the in-depth stage of the audit. Additionally, the auditor can always refer to the survey memorandum if the question ever arises as to why a particular department was selected over another.

Even if the auditor feels strongly that he knows where the problems lie, he should still not voice an opinion at this stage of the audit. Following the in-depth stage of the audit the operations auditor will be given an opportunity to voice an opinion. By then, all of the evidence will have been analyzed. Therefore, the auditor must use due care to see that the survey memorandum is used only as an audit tool and not as an official report of the audit.

The In-Depth Audit

The in-depth audit consists of an extensive search for the facts. An extensive search for facts is a time-consuming process. Therefore, only one department is initially audited during the in-depth stage of an operations audit. The results of the preliminary stage are used to select the one department where it is most obvious that problems exist. The auditor's objective during the in-depth stage of the audit is to uncover the causes of these problems.

During the in-depth stage of the audit, the operations auditor compiles views, suggestions, comments, and trends. The primary tool for all of this is a questionnaire interview of departmental employees. The auditor will usually utilize the questionnaire with most or all of the employees in the department being audited.

Although the use of questionnaires comprises a major portion of the in-depth stage of the operations audit, the auditor will also learn from observation. Chapter 5 examines the in-depth stage of the operations audit in detail and discusses the departmental questionnaires that form the major audit tool used in the in-depth audit.

The Audit Report

Once the in-depth stage of the audit has been completed, the auditor is ready to prepare an audit report. The audit report consists of a written summary of the auditor's scope, the findings, and should define the problems that have been uncovered (see Appendix G for an illustration). The audit report normally gives examples of specific problems where changes in management practices might be most easily implemented. Even though the audit report is the final step of the in-depth audit, it is best to not wait until the last minute to begin preparing the report. "The auditor will be well advised to start it on the first day; the surest way to drag it out is to wait until the end of the study."[15]

The Recommended Operations Audit Model

A complete operations audit model for a small general hospital has been described in this chapter. Figure 4-1 schematically illustrates the complete model in a format that portrays all of the various interrelationships. This model can be summarized in the following manner. The industry through averages, and the individual hospital through goals, objectives, and budgets provide the criteria against which the auditor measures the hospital being audited. The auditor obtains the data by which to measure against the established criteria by taking a physical tour, acquiring written documentation, interviewing managers and department heads, and by analyzing several financial ratios and statistics. On the basis of this data, the auditor compiles a survey memorandum that isolates one department for an in-depth audit. The auditor then goes into that individual department and makes an extensive search for facts. This search for facts centers primarily around questionnaire interviews of those individuals working in the department being audited. Once the auditor has completed the in-depth audit of a department, he prepares a report of his findings. Copies of the audit report go to top management and the management of the department that was audited.

Figure 4-2 provides an internal viewpoint of the actions that appear on the far left side of Figure 4-1. Figure 4-2 can be viewed as a submodel of Figure 4-1 since Figure 4-2 involves a more specific look at the generalized steps shown in the earlier exhibit.

With the operations audit model described in this chapter to use as a guide, a qualified operations auditor should have no difficulty in performing such an audit at a small, general hospital. The framework that the model provides, along with the accompanying questionnaires, permits a systemized study of problems in six hospital departments.

Summary

Although operations auditing has been defined as the application of common sense to a business situation, there is still a need for the auditor to have some type of format to follow when performing an operations audit. A lack of uniformity among firms and a lack of interest among researchers has resulted in little work in the area of operations audit models. There is adequate uniformity

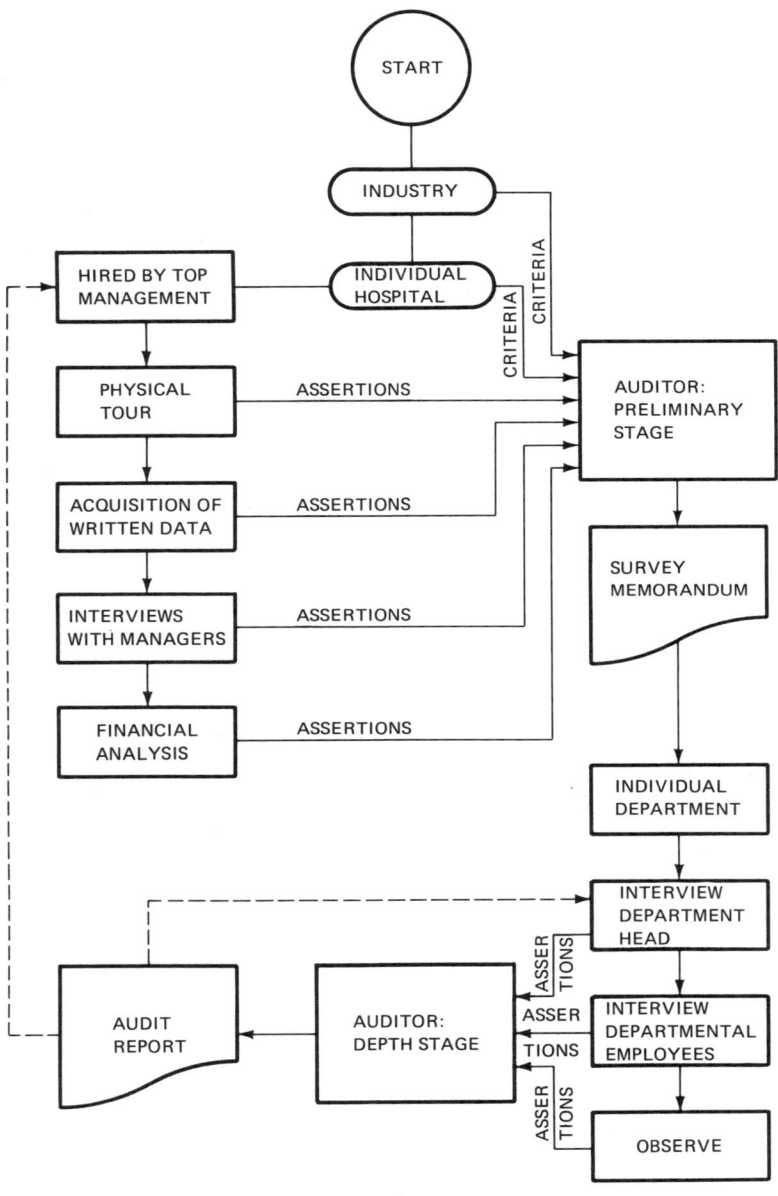

Figure 4-1. Operations Audit Model.

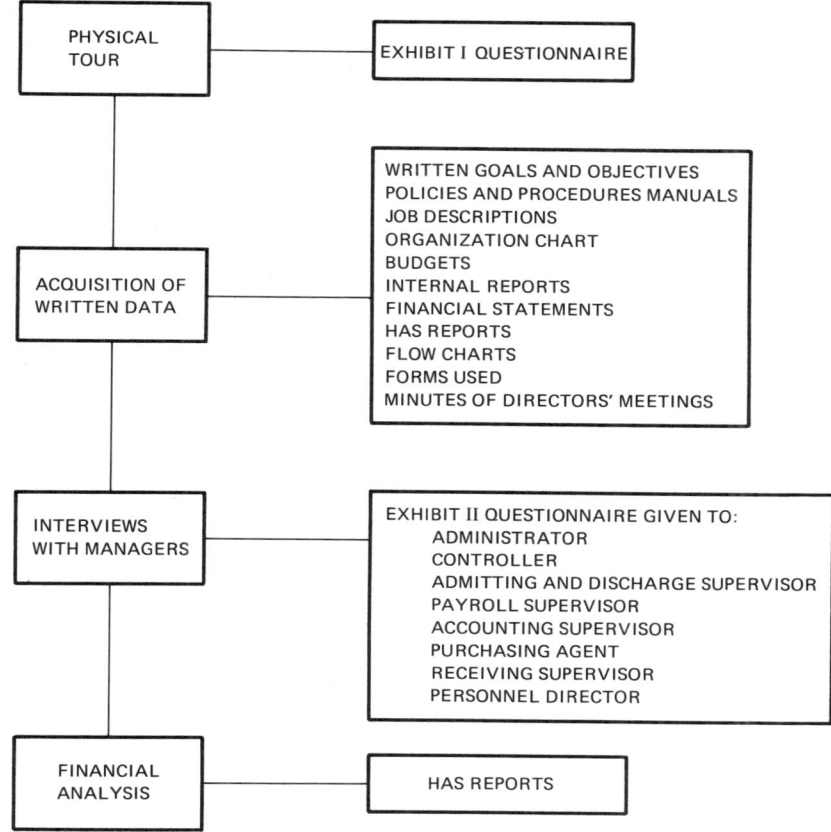

Figure 4-2. Operations Audit Model—Specific Sources.

among hospitals, however, to warrant the expenditure of the time and effort necessary to prepare an operations audit model for that type of business.

This chapter has described an operations audit model for six key departments in a small, general hospital. Each of the steps in the model has been explained and justified. Although this researcher has no way of knowing whether this is the best possible operations audit model for a hospital, it has proven, through use in two operations audits, to be a workable, useful model (see Appendix G for further information regarding the actual audits). A qualified operations auditor, even though he might never have performed a hospital operations audit, should find the model and accompanying questionnaires to be useful guides in the performance of an operations audit.

5

Model In-Depth Audits

Patient Census Management (Admissions and Discharges) Department

The processing of hospital admissions and discharges is probably the most important aspect of operating a hospital. It is the responsibility of the admissions group to admit patients, obtain all necessary personal information from the patient, and to determine how the patient's bill is to be paid. Although this is a necessary function, it is often bypassed by those patients who enter through the emergency room. In many hospitals these emergency cases (or pseudo-emergencies) may account for nearly half of the patients admitted.

Hospital bed capacity is an important aspect of the work of those individuals working in the area of patient census management. The admissions group is responsible for keeping all beds filled in order to maximize income, while at the same time, it is the responsibility of the discharge group to keep adequate empty beds available for use by incoming emergencies. Additionally, the admissions group is responsible for maintaining a profitable patient mix. Most hospitals cannot prosper only from room charges. If all beds were occupied by patients recovering from surgery who need only to rest, the hospital would be operating at a loss. Only when patients are available who require special services for which extra charges can be made will a hospital be profitable (or break even).[1] Therefore, the admissions group should schedule patients so that there is always a broad mix of patient services being performed. It is only through close cooperation with medical doctors that the personnel of patient census management can achieve the objectives of the organization.

Besides maintaining a full hospital with a profitable patient mix, it is also the responsibility of the admissions and discharge groups to collect from patients for services rendered. The admissions group has the responsibility of determining how a bill is expected to be paid. If a third party payer such as an insurance company, Medicare, workman's compensation, or other group is responsible for the bill, then the admissions group is responsible for obtaining all facts and information such as company name, policy number, and extent of benefits. If the bill is to be paid by the patient, or at least partially by the patient, there is usually an attempt to make the collection in advance of performing the services. The discharge group is responsible for collecting those bills that are not paid in advance.

A hospital can normally not refuse to serve a patient without insurance who will not pay in advance, but the knowledge that a particular patient is not apt to pay gives the discharge group adequate opportunity to try and collect from welfare programs or other sources. Secondly, it encourages a reasonably quick discharge of the indigent patient (perhaps to another health care facility, or to be treated as an outpatient).

An operations audit of the patient census management area of a hospital is a beneficial tool to the organization. There have been numerous articles written on various aspects of admissions and discharges and there are many examples of well-run facilities. These articles and questionnaire responses from hospital department heads were used in the preparation of audit questions that examine the area of patient census management with the objective of finding problems, or the lack thereof. These questions, which appear in Appendix A, are designed so that most can be answered by "yes" or "no" answers. A "no" answer is an indication to the auditor that a problem area exists. (See Appendix A for the original questions as well as the ranking of their importance by the hospital patient census managers surveyed in this study.) The questions that require a more complete answer (such as turnover rate, absenteeism, and types of reports prepared) will have to be examined more closely by the auditor to determine whether a problem area does in fact exist.

Again, it should be noted that the questionnaire is to be administered to more than one employee in any department. The fact that the auditor receives different answers indicates a problem. A few of the questions can be answered by the auditor through observation, but he may wish to corroborate his own observations with the questionnaire results.

The questions on the Patient Census Management Department Questionnaire (see Appendix A) have been divided into seven categories (Formal Policies and Procedures, Financial Considerations, Census Management, Physical Facilities, Budgets, Communications, and Personnel). The questions relating to formal policies and procedures are simply to determine whether or not there is any form of written documentation concerning the operations performed within the department and whether such policies and procedures are followed. The availability of a policies and procedures manual is advantageous when new employees are hired or when questions arise for which there is no precedent. A formal manual gives employees a better understanding of what is to be accomplished and the means of accomplishing these objectives.[2]

The questions in the section on financial considerations involve the financial status of the patients. Of primary importance is whether a written financial policy exists. Patients can sometimes be induced to pay at a specified time if they are told what the hospital's financial policy is.

Questions 6 through 15 relate to the collection for billed services. Receivables are the largest single asset for many hospitals, and bad debt expense is one of the largest single expenses. For these reasons, it is essential that a hospital take every conceivable step in order to collect from patients as soon as possible. This can involve accepting only those elective patients who are financially secure (questions 6 and 7) or it can involve getting the money immediately from other sources (questions 8-11). Patients without cash may be willing to have their charges put on a credit card as they leave the hospital. The hospital will then have its money and a bank has the problem of collecting from the patient. The acceptance by hospitals of charge cards serves the dual purpose of speeding up cash flow and eliminating bad debts. The remaining questions in this section examine other causes of potential noncollection. Questions 13 and 14 are designed to examine whether an employee is capable of knowing when an insurance policy is invalid or does not apply in a given situation.

The final question of the section is important in that many times a patient believes that he has paid his bill in full, only to receive an additional billing a few weeks later. The former patient then becomes confused or irritated, or both, and there are lengthy delays in receiving payment.

The questions in the census management category involve nonfinancial contact with patients. A hospital must maintain a high patient count in order to maximize revenues while at the same time, several beds must remain unoccupied in order to allow for emergency admissions. Most of the questions in this section relate to that balance in the number of patients on hand.

Questions 27 and 28 are for the purpose of determining whether the admissions forms in use are adequate for the purpose for which they are intended.

Question 35 concerning pseudo-emergencies is related to hospital income in that a reduction in emergency room cases normally results in a reduction in bad debts. Emergency room cases are not handled procedurally by the admissions department in the same manner as nonemergency cases. Consequently, it is easier for emergency room patients to avoid paying their bills.[3]

The section of the questionnaire on physical facilities is appropriate for any department. Without adequate facilities, employees cannot operate at their full potential. If there are excessive facilities then the hospital is misusing its resources. The only question in the physical facilities section that deserves a separate explanation is question 45. Each admitting and discharge officer needs a private office since they will be discussing personal financial matters with patients. A patient is often reluctant to talk about financial problems when there are other patients nearby.

The questionnaire section relating to budgets examines how aware employees are of the budget and the corresponding budget variances. Since a budget is a quantitative expression of hospital goals and objectives, it is important that employees be knowledgeable about the budget. In effect, the budget is a total model of the entire organization. The lack of a budget, or the lack of knowledge about a budget, is an indication that employees do not know the established goals.

Communication between departments and individuals is as important in hospitals as in any other organization. An employee's ability to create are based upon what has been communicated to him. For these reasons, the questions in the section on communication are designed to determine whether communication exists. The last question in the section (60) attempts to determine whether the entire business office is communicating its story to the public.

The questionnaire section relating to personnel is a broad one that examines the loyalty and training of departmental employees. Job descriptions (question 61) show the duties, responsibilities and work performed for each job position. Job descriptions are helpful in personnel selection, promotions, and acquainting new employees with their jobs.

Questions 63, 64, and 80 deal with employee loyalty. Just the ability to answer questions 63 and 64 on turnover and absence is indicative of an awareness of the problem.

The adequacy of staff size is the major emphasis of questions 68 through 75. The number of employees should be commensurate with the work load. In some locales the hospital is a seasonal business. If this is true, there should be some scaling down of staff during the off-season. This could be accomplished by utilizing temporary employees during the busy season.

Questions 78 and 79 relate to employee input. If the system is conducive to suggestions from employees (and others), there is greater opportunity for new ideas to surface.

The management of hospital admissions and discharges is a many faceted job. Patients are more influenced by events in this department than any other area of the business office. If the business office has a favorable public relations image, it is most likely attributable to patients having a positive image of the patient census management area.

Personnel Department

A hospital is composed of people who provide their services. Without these people, a hospital cannot be successful. The skill, enthusiasm, and satisfaction of employees is a necessity. Since a hospital is composed of so many varying job positions, it is necessary that a separate department exist to hire employees and coordinate employee relations.

Personnel work is neither welfare nor necessary overhead. Modern personnel management is concerned with maximizing the effectiveness of the work force through application of sound and proved personnel policies and practices. It gives full recognition to the influence of the human element in achieving objectives and in gaining the overall success of the enterprise. Furthermore, personnel work is of a continuous type. It cannot be practiced only one hour each day or one day a week. Personnel management requires a constant alertness and awareness to human relations and their importance in everyday operations.[4]

The Personnel Department Questionnaire for the in-depth audit is illustrated in Appendix B. The questions are categorized into five sections (General, Clerical Operations, Departmental Staff, Physical Facilities, and Communication).

The general questions are designed to determine the nature of the personnel function in a particular hospital. The answers to the first three questions, plus 6 and 7, will give the auditor insight as to where the personnel function stands in relation to other hospital departments. Questions 4, 5 and 8 basically ask whether or not the personnel department employees have an idea as to what it is they are supposed to be accomplishing.

Questions 9 through 12 deal with personnel policies. It is not only essential that policies exist, but that employees be aware of such policies. If well-known policies exist, then problems can be solved when no precedent exists, and different persons will be able to come to identical conclusions in resolving personnel matters.

Questions 15, 27, 29, 30, and 37 relate to the problem of a position being unfilled. If the personnel department is aware of these statistics, then the problem is partially solved.

The training and education of hospital employees is examined by questions 32, 33, and 34. If a hospital does not encourage its employees to improve themselves, it cannot be expected that many employees will participate in educational activities on their own initiative.

The remainder of the questions in the general section involve relations with hospital employees, particularly the problems of treating all workers equally and paying an adequate salary. If a hospital cannot answer "yes" to these questions, it may suddenly find itself in the middle of a problem. Recent unionization drives in hospitals are as much based on unfair treatment of certain employees as on low salaries.[5]

The section of the questionnaire on clerical operations relates to the activities performed within the personnel department. The record keeping that is necessary results in a great deal of paper flow. Questions 40, 41, and 49 through 52 pertain to the quality and quantity of records kept. The personnel department should be a source of information on any topic concerning an employee. If the hospital has to answer "no" to one of these questions, then total information would not be available.

Questions 42 through 45 involve forms that are used. Inconvenience is often caused by having to use several forms when one well-designed form could be used in the same situation.

Questions 46 and 47 on the topic of filing are indicative of whether or not a personnel department is properly staffed with well-trained employees. Filing is an easy chore to avoid when other work is more imminent.

Question 53 asks whether references are checked before an applicant is hired. The personnel department will often avoid future problems for other departments by following through on reference checks. This procedure is easy to overlook when a position has to be filled in a hurry.

The section on departmental staff relates to staff size and the competency of personnel employees. Personnel department employees must not only be knowledgeable about hospital personnel policies and fringe benefits, but also various laws such as FICA, EEO, and minimum-wage requirements.

Only question 64 in this section involves other departments. If the personnel department is aware of employee turnover in other departments, then steps can be taken to eliminate the high turnover problems.

The section of the questionnaire relating to physical facilities is similar to the section in the previous illustrated questionnaire for patient census management. Questions 68 and 69 are especially appropriate for a personnel department since the department will be most valuable to employees if it is easily accessible to them.

The final section of the Personnel Department Questionnaire relates to communication. This is the most important section since it is imperative that the department communicate constantly with all other departments and with individual employees. The personnel department is normally a staff function, and as such, it exists only to help others. Without two-way communication the personnel department can be of help to no one. Questions 80, 81, and 88 through 91 are concerned with the personnel department's communication with other departments.

The remaining questions in the communication section apply to communication with individual employees. In many situations, the only contact an employee has with top management is through the personnel department. The personnel department should be the one place where an employee can go with a grievance, suggestion, or question. A "house organ," suggestion box, and a frequently-used bulletin board facilitate communication.

The personnel department plays an important role at a hospital. If the department can answer "yes" to the questions on the questionnaire, it has few problems and is providing the benefits for which the department was established.

Accounting Department

As discussed in Chapter 3, the accounting department in hospitals has long been a luxury rather than a necessity. Until recently, there were no generally accepted accounting principles for hospitals. Generally accepted accounting principles were not needed since rarely was there a need to refer to the financial statements. Anyone with a knowledge of bookkeeping could perform the necessary tasks. The past decade, however, has witnessed a change in hospital accounting. New laws require greater accuracy in that new guidelines for reporting now exist that were not required previously. New sources of financing require greater emphasis on the preparation of financial statements.

The additional work that has been created for the hospital accountant in the past decade has caused poor management practices to arise. Hospital accountants have noted increases in paperwork. This has left little time for reference to overall goals and objectives. The operations audit Accounting Department Questionnaire (illustrated in Appendix C) is divided into five sections (General, Budgets, Internal Control, Procedures, and Departmental Staff).

The general section begins with questions pertaining to operating procedures. The lack of established procedures would be a real hindrance when new employees are hired. Question 5, asking about the existence of an organization chart, falls into the same category since the organization chart would answer the questions not only of new employees, but those of the old employees as well.

Questions 3, 4, 6, 7, 10, and 15 relate to the quality of the reports prepared by the accounting department. Financial reports must be user oriented. Financial data approaches worthlessness if it is not provided quickly. Reports must provide usable information and provide it quickly.

Communication between departments is the subject of question 9. Accounting is a language, but there is little value in knowing the language if others do not use the same language.

Questions 11 through 14 examine the adequacy of facilities. Since the accounting department has only recently been recognized for its true worth, there is danger that the department may have been slighted when facilities were provided.

The last two questions of the general section examine the amount of receivables and uncollectible accounts. If the volume of receivables is on the uptrend, or if the number of days of revenue in receivables is above average, then perhaps the accounting department is not devoting enough time to pressuring patients for payment.

The section of the questionnaire concerning budgets should be informative to the auditor in a general way. The mere existence of a budget is indicative that some planning and looking ahead is being performed. Question 21 extends the subject of budgets to the aspect of who actually prepares the budget. Employees should have the opportunity to participate in the preparation of a budget. Question 27 is a natural outgrowth of the existence of a budget, but is occasionally ignored. A budget is really two tools. It is a planning tool, and it is also a control tool. Little additional effort is necessary to utilize the second tool after the first one is carefully developed.

The final question in the budget section relates to the size of the accounting department budget. This is probably a worthless question since experience seems to indicate that few department heads ever feel that their budget is large enough.

The internal control section of the accounting questionnaire involves a great deal of overlap with the hospital financial audit. The CPA firm that performs the annual financial audit is supposed to verify the existence of internal control.[6] However, the financial auditor may not always insist that a problem of internal control be corrected. Instead, the financial auditor may extend his audit procedures to assure himself that the problem of internal control has not caused another problem. For this reason, the section on internal control is included in the operations audit questionnaire. If the CPA firm that performs the annual financial audit also does the operations audit, the auditors may already be familiar with the internal control system. It should be noted that the purpose of an internal control system is not solely to prevent employee fraud. An internal control system is also designed to catch errors as they happen (rather than waiting until year end for the auditor to make the correction) and to ascertain whether the goals and objectives of management are being reached.

The section of the questionnaire relating to procedures involves indicators of problems within the accounting department. Additionally, the accounting department problems can lead to problems in other departments as well. For example, questions 50 through 52 involve when—and how quickly—financial statements are prepared. If the accounting department does not provide reports often enough or quickly enough, other departments could be adversely affected due to the lack of information. Question 56 examines the quality of internal reports as presented to the users.

Questions 54, 55, and 57 examine the possibility that the accounting department might be doing more work than is necessary.

Questions 58 and 59 ask about purchase discounts. A hospital that does not take advantage of all cash discounts is effectively paying an excessively high interest rate.

Questions 60 through 64 pertain to subsidiary ledgers. One advantage of using subsidiary ledgers is that the system provides immediate notification if an error has been made. However, if the subsidiary ledgers are never reconciled with the control accounts, the advantage offered by subsidiary ledgers is lost.

Question 65 asks if depreciation is recorded in the hospital accounts. Surprisingly, this question pertains to proper cash management. Unlike most businesses, hospitals are required by law (Medicare) to put aside cash equal to depreciation expense. If the hospital does not record depreciation, it probably means that no cash was available.

Questions 66 through 73 relate primarily to the management of cash flows. With the exception of questions 72 and 73, all of these questions pertain to getting the inflows to come in more promptly.

The final question in this section relates to the ageless problem of whether anyone tries to control the cost of the copying machine.

The last section of the accounting questionnaire concerns departmental staffing. As discussed earlier in this chapter, job descriptions are necessary if positions are to be filled or employees want to know the scope of their job.

Questions 76, 79, 81, and 84 relate to the qualifications of the accounting staff. Hospital accountants need the same types of knowledge as accountants in private industrial firms. Since hospitals have often paid lower salaries than industrial firms, it has been possible for them to hire individuals who only had a small amount of accounting background. Question 85 is similar to the above since it is necessary to pay competitive wages to hire and hold good people.

The encouragement of continuing education is examined in questions 91 and 92. With the constant change in laws affecting hospitals, it is a necessity for hospital accountants to participate in a great deal of continuing education. If the hospital does not encourage employees to continue their educations, there is less chance that it will take place.

The final question (Does the hospital have an internal auditor?) is difficult to explain. It was somewhat surprising to this writer that the question received a high enough importance rating to stay on the operations audit questionnaire. Apparently, accounting department heads have heard about the value and contributions of internal auditors. However, the internal auditor must be paid a salary and the cost/benefit ratio may not be favorable in the small hospital (as was discussed in Chapter 2).

The accounting department is actually the core of the hospital business office. If the accounting department performs its job well, other departments will benefit.

Payroll Department

The hospital payroll department is the one department with which all hospital employees are experts. If the payroll department makes an error, someone (or everyone) is going to find out about it. Since the duties of the payroll department are of a constantly recurring nature, a small problem can often be quite costly over a year's time. The operations audit Payroll Department Questionnaire (see Appendix D) consists of five sections (Controls, Procedures, Physical Facilities, Personnel, and General).

The section on internal controls involves a great deal of overlap with the internal control testing that occurs during the annual financial audit (as was true with the previously discussed accounting questionnaire). It is with sections such as this that one can observe the close relationship between the operations audit and the financial audit. The operations audit would make a perfect adjunct to the annual financial audit.

The procedures section of the payroll department's questionnaire is important due to the constant recurrence of the procedures performed. Question 20 is the most important as far as employees are concerned. A "no" answer will not pinpoint the cause of the problem, but it will certainly indicate a problem worth investigating. Question 21 might explain the reason why the payroll is not prepared on time. The delay in the receipt of time cards causes the entire payroll system to balk.

Questions 22, 28, and 29 inquire into compliance with federal laws. If reports and payments are not made on time, the organization is subject to penalties.

Question 30 explores the possibility that the delay in filing quarterly reports might be due to delays in the secretarial pool or a lack of typists.

The possibility of further reducing payroll preparation costs is examined in questions 24 and 25. Obviously, payroll costs could be reduced if employees were paid less often. Admittedly, this is often difficult since once a payroll routine is established, it is difficult to change since the changeover period is often a burden on the employee.

Questions 26 and 27 are intended to explore the use of payroll department reports. Gross payroll, by department, is useful for managers since it makes them aware of the cost of department activity.

Communication is the subject of question 31. Since the payroll department performs work for all other departments, it is essential that the payroll employees remain alert to problems in other departments that affect payroll.

The final questions relate to overtime. With the time constraints that exist in the preparation of payroll, it would be possible that recurring overtime (at premium rates) might be relied upon in order to complete the payroll on time. Overtime costs a hospital 50 percent more than straight time and should be avoided. A hospital should consider adding a second shift or utilizing temporary employees rather than pay the overtime premium.

The physical facilities category of the questionnaire inquires as to whether enough equipment is available and whether all equipment available is being utilized. Question 40 examines the possibility that storage space is being wasted on supplies that will never be used. It is often difficult to convince people that expensive supplies should be scrapped, but they are a sunk cost. If supplies will not likely be used, then they should be disposed of.

The questions in the personnel category are similar to those in the same section of the previously discussed accounting questionnaire. The only major difference is with respect to questions 49 and 50. Since the jobs performed in the department often vary from one day to the next, it has been suggested by some department heads that payroll employees could transfer to other departments on slow days. Whereas on busy days, employees from other departments could transfer to payroll. However, there is a great deal of diversity of opinion on this topic as can be seen by referring to the importance ranking of these items in Appendix D. Although the idea seems good in theory, some department heads indicated that the constant transferring could cause morale problems that might result in additional problems rather than solving problems.

The general category consists of several miscellaneous concepts. Questions 55 and 58 relate to procedures manuals and job descriptions. It is important that these be in writing so that there will be less chance of misinterpretation.

Questions 57 and 60 relate to the reports prepared by the department. No department should lose sight of the fact that reports are prepared for the user. Therefore, it is necessary that the preparer have an awareness of what the user needs. Questions 61 and 62 pertain to the data recorded in the payroll records.

The forms should be designed to accommodate all information that is needed, but only the information that is needed.

Questions 63 through 66 are rather sophisticated in that analysis is frequently necessary to determine the best course of action. Since workman's compensation rates are subject to merit reductions, and hospitals have the ability to treat patients, it seems reasonable that many occurrences of injury could be treated by the hospital without notifying the workman's compensation carrier.

One of the most important questions is probably number 67. Errors have to be corrected, and corrections create problems. When an error is made in the preparation of a paycheck, there is the additional cost of writing a second check plus the employees' loss of confidence in the payroll department.

The payroll department comes in contact with all hospital employees. Consequently, the employees' image of the payroll department often becomes their image of the entire hospital business office. Therefore, for public relations reasons, it is paramount that the payroll department operate with as few problems as possible.

Purchasing Department

The responsibility of the purchasing department is defined as the obtaining of materials, equipment and supplies of the right quality, in the right quantity, at the right price, delivered at the proper time. The procurement of supplies is a major business function in a hospital since it is necessary to coordinate the needs of many diverse departments with the offerings of numerous sellers. Because of the cumulative effects of any savings that can be accomplished in the purchasing department, an operations audit should be of as great a value in the purchasing department as in any other area of the hospital. The operations audit Purchasing Department Questionnaire (see Appendix E) consists of questions divided into six sections (General, Communication, Policies and Procedures, Departmental Staff, Relations with Vendors, and Forms and Reports).

The general section begins with questions relating to the overall aspect of the purchasing department. Questions 2, 3, and 13, in particular, emphasize the fact that a purchasing department must be user oriented.

Questions 5, 12, and 20 inquire as to whether there is any type of inventory control system that the purchasing agent can use as a guide in buying. The purchasing agent must understand that excessive inventories cost the hospital money in the form of storage costs and interest. Question 8 goes along with the objective of minimizing inventories in that one generic product can often be used for several departments instead of purchasing different brand name items for each user.

The subject of cost records is the topic of questions 10, 14, and 16. The availability of such records is a major consideration in determining problem situations.

Questions 15 and 22 relate to policies and perhaps should be included in a subsequent section of this questionnaire. Question 22 is particularly important for internal control reasons.

Question 17 pertains to the existence of a product evaluation committee. Such a committee is beneficial in that individuals from user departments are given the opportunity to evaluate products. This provides quality guidelines for the purchasing agent.

Questions 11, 19, 23, and 24 are for the purpose of examining the adequacy of the physical facilities of the department. Question 11 involves the availability of vendor catalogs and price lists. The lack of a library of such materials may be evidence that the purchasing department is not performing enough exploratory work prior to placing orders.

Question 21 looks at the problem of employee evaluation. One measure of purchasing agent performance is the price variance. If the purchasing agent knows that price variances will be computed, there is incentive to find the lowest costs possible consistent with quality.

The section of the questionnaire on the topic of communication is important since all work performed by the purchasing department is for the benefit of other departments. It is especially important that an open channel of communication is maintained with receiving and accounting. A good internal control system requires that accounting receive copies of requisitions and purchase orders before an invoice is paid. Consequently, the purchasing department must deliver documents to accounting on a regular basis. The final question in the section relating to the budgets of other departments (if answered "yes") gives the purchasing department the opportunity to act as a control step to keep departments from overspending.

The section on policies and procedures begins by asking whether a formal manual exists. The existence of a policies and procedures manual helps to insure consistency of action among various employees. Questions 30 through 34 continue the topic of departmental policies. Question 31, in particular, should be emphasized since the purchase of capital equipment involves a long-range decision that differs from the routine purchase of supplies.

Question 35 attempts to determine where purchases are made on a haphazard basis, or whether some system has been devised that is intended to minimize inventory storing and ordering costs. Question 37 has been devised with the same intent except that out-of-stock costs are also to be considered. Questions 52 and 53 also relate to the reduction of carrying costs.

The subject of quantity discounts is examined in questions 39 and 40. Simply because a hospital is small does not mean that it could not obtain discounts for buying in large quantities. Several hospitals could, for example, take advantage of quantity discounts by pooling orders with other hospitals in the same locale.

Questions 41 through 45 pertain to the efforts made by the purchasing department to obtain items at the lowest available cost consistent with required quality. The auditor should assure himself that the obtaining of bids and quotations is a constantly recurring procedure. It is easy to overlook the procedures after suppliers for all products have been established.

A value judgment is required of the purchasing staff in question 46. Purchasing agents are often asked to order specific quantities of certain items. Occasionally, these requests are for excessive quantitites and the excess ends up as obsolete inventory.

Question 47 asks whether several sources of supply are maintained. As can be seen in Appendix E, there was a great deal of difference of opinion on this question. Some purchasing agents felt this was an important question since the shutdown of one supplier could present problems for the hospital. Other purchasing agents felt this question was of little importance. Apparently this latter group felt that low prices were more important than an assured source of supply.

Questions 48 and 49 inquire as to whether anything is done when orders are not shipped immediately. Follow-up is necessary since problems are often incurred as a result of late deliveries.

Questions 50 and 51 pertain to purchase prices. If purchase prices are not included on orders, there is danger that a higher price might be charged. The final question of the section could apply to any department. Files should be periodically purged of old records. The records should at least be removed to a record storage room rather than continue to be maintained in the filing cabinets within the department.

The section of the questionnaire on departmental staff is somewhat similar to the same section of previously discussed questionnaires. The major difference from earlier questionnaires relates to questions 58 and 59. Purchasing department employees must make a conscious effort to keep abreast of products if they are going to properly serve the hospital.

Since purchasing employees have a great deal of contact with vendors, it is imperative that good relations are maintained. Questions 63, 64, and 66 deal with the reputation of vendors—that is, whether the vendors will back their products and whether vendors can be depended upon to perform in various situations. If vendors cannot be depended upon, the hospital may find itself in a dangerous out-of-stock situation.

Question 65 inquires as to whether a purchasing policy statement is made available to vendors. The availability of such a statement can reduce the amount of time that has to be spent talking to vendors. Question 67 has the same objective (that of reducing the time spent with salesmen) except that it asks whether an attempt is made to keep vendors from bothering other department heads.

The final question of this section is very important. There should be a definite policy with respect to the acceptance of gifts from vendors. Obviously, there is a very fine line of distinction between what might be considered as a gift and that which might be considered as a kickback.

The section of the questionnaire concerning forms and reports is similar to preceding questionnaires with the emphasis on size and spacing. Question 72 is significant in that the availability of preprinted bid and quotation forms may be indicative that the forms are regularly used for the purposes for which they were intended.

The hospital purchasing department serves only for the benefit of other departments. If the purchasing department can improve its management practices, the end result may be cost savings in all departments. Purchasing is closely related to the entire area of materials management. Consequently, some of the questions on the operations audit questionnaire for purchasing overlap with certain questions on the questionnaire designed for receiving and materials handling. This overlap is necessary since the organization of departments in the area of materials management differs among hospitals.

Receiving and Materials Handling Department

The final departmental questionnaire has been designed for use in the area of receiving and materials handling. This department's questionnaire (shown in Appendix F) is divided into five sections (General, Procedures, Departmental Personnel, Physical Facilities, and Forms and Reports).

The general section begins with inquiries as to whether there is a receiving department and whether such a department is properly used. If some goods that come into the hospital bypass the receiving department, there are probably unnecessary costs incurred in tracking down whether a delivery was ever made. A good internal control system requires that merchandise not be paid for until a receiving report is on file. If a shipment is delivered directly to the user, that receiving report is not prepared.

Questions 3, 18, and 23 through 25 relate to communication with other departments. The area of receiving and materials handling is strictly a service department and to be useful, it must be responsive to user needs.

Questions 4 through 7 pertain to the accessibility of goods kept in the storeroom. If a system has been designed for storing of supplies, there is greater ease in finding requested items. Convenience is also a consideration in question 8. It is impractical to have shipments unloaded at one location and then have to pay someone to carry the items to the other end of the hospital.

The subject of inventory control is examined in questions 9 through 13. An important ingredient in materials handling is the realization that carrying inventories is costly. Sound management requires that inventories be kept at the lowest possible level subject to the constraint that out-of-stock situations do not occur.

Questions 14 and 15 inquire as to whether the department head is familiar with his operating costs. If the receiving department is not provided with cost figures, there is no way the department head can determine whether problems exist.

Questions 16, 17, and 19 through 21 relate to the accuracy of the perpetual inventory system. Most hospitals check the accuracy of the perpetual system with at least an annual physical count. Any reconciliation between the two inventories should be small. Otherwise, the perpetual system is not serving the purposes for which it was designed and, therefore, should be eliminated or more attention paid to its successful operation.

The topic of whether inventories are insured is asked in question 22. If a large amount of assets are kept in one location, the hospital should at least explore the possibility of insuring the items.

The questionnaire section on procedures begins with questions inquiring as to whether a formal set of procedures have been set down in writing. Questions 29 through 33 pertain primarily to relations with vendors and freight lines. It is important that the receiving employees assure themselves as to product quantity and quality before accepting delivery. Otherwise, the hospital may find that it has been shorted, or that damaged merchandise has been accepted.

The subject of whether material requisitions are required is explored in question 35. The use of requisitions is not only important for charging costs to user departments, but is also an internal control device in that any decrease in inventory must be matched by a requisition. Question 37 examines the problem of whether there are only certain individuals who are authorized to submit requisitions.

Question 36 explores the question of whether catalog numbers have been assigned to products stocked. If so, requisitions of materials can be accurately accounted for.

By asking question 39, the auditor may be able to determine what happens to supplies after they leave the storeroom. There should be some provision for immediate return to the storeroom of those items that are not going to be used by the original requisitioning department.

Questions 40 through 43 and 45 relate to relations with user departments. It is usually much more practical to deliver to specific departments only on certain days rather than to have to run to every department everyday. Supplies that are used regularly can even be automatically delivered at regular intervals.

Question 46 merely requires a value judgment as to whether the filing system is satisfactory. The auditor may have the opportunity to observe the answer to this question.

The remainder of the questions in the procedures section of the questionnaire pertain to the problem of inventory carrying costs. Employees are often reluctant to dispose of obsolete supplies since the supplies used to be valuable. The accounting concept of sunk costs is often difficult to grasp, but obsolete inventories are a perfect example and therefore should be disposed of at the earliest possible date.

The section of questions regarding departmental personnel is much like the similarly titled section in previous questionnaires. Justification for these questions can be obtained by referring to the previous questionnaires.

The physical facilities questions are particularly important for the receiving department, particularly the questions relating to the size of the department. "No" answers to the questions on storage space and width of aisles could mean that the department employees have a problem in handling inventory to their satisfaction. Questions 69 and 70 are important since most of the assets in the department would be subject to loss by fire or theft. It must be remembered that the availability of physical space is one of the services offered by the receiving department. Thus, physical facilities should be strongly emphasized.

The final section probes the topic of receiving reports and requisition forms. If the forms do not contain sufficient space, employees will spend excessive amounts of time just trying to write small enough to utilize the forms. Additionally, there is less chance of errors if forms contain a full description of the materials being requested.

Summary

This chapter has basically described the departmental questionnaires that would be used during the in-depth stage of a hospital operations audit. The comments have been made to illustate the reasoning behind each of the questions. If used in conjunction with the operations audit model discussed in Chapter 4, the questionnaires are a valuable operations audit tool.

6 Conclusion

Summary

Hospitals have grown considerably in recent years, primarily as a result of an increase in the availability of third-party payers. As a result of this growth and the ability to pass costs on to someone other than the patient, hospitals have encountered serious operating problems. This has been complicated by the problem that measuring the standards for hospital managers has never been an easy task since most hospitals, by definition, are nonprofit institutions.

Accordingly, hospitals are prime subjects for the use of the technique of operations auditing. Operations auditing is a systematized search for operating problems. Profit-seeking firms can often recognize the existence of problems through changes in contribution margin and other financial statement figures. For hospitals, however, it is necessary to actively look for problems. An individual, or team of individuals, can go into a hospital and, through observation and analysis of internal data, identify areas where costs can be reduced without reducing hospital effectiveness.

The majority of hospitals are fairly small and cannot afford to hire a full-time internal operations auditor. Consequently, these small hospitals must rely on CPA firms or other outside auditors to perform operations audit engagements. CPA firms should be desirous of performing operations audits for hospitals for a number of reasons. First, the operations audit would result in increased billings, and the work could be performed during what might otherwise be a slack period for the firm. Second, the operations audit would tie in closely with the annual financial audit. In fact, some observations might be made during the financial audit that could provide a starting point in an operations audit. Third, an operations audit could lead to an engagement for the management services department of the CPA firm. It must be remembered that an operations audit is only a problem-finding device; it is not a problem-solving device. The management services staff would be in a good position to provide the problem-solving expertise. Finally, the CPA firm could find that its public relations image would be improved as a result of performing an operations audit at a hospital. At a time when many professional accountants are concerned with the phrase "social accounting," hospital operations audits provide a golden opportunity. What could be a more perfect example of "social accounting" than for a CPA firm to point out areas where the local hospital could reduce its operating problems. The opportunity to perform a hospital operations audit would permit CPA firms to prove that "social accounting" was more than just a phrase.

In order to simplify the process of performing an operations audit at a hospital, the auditor should have available a detailed model, complete with questionnaires, that would provide a guide in the performance of an operations audit. Within this volume, the various steps of an operations audit have been structured to form that complete model, and an attempt has been made to justify each and every step of the procedure.

The research that provided the basis for the operations auditing model represents a compilation of the knowledge of hospital department heads and managers. These individuals are knowledgeable on how hospitals should be operated, and their contributions facilitated compiling an exhaustive list of areas of possible problems in six hospital departments (accounting, payroll, patient census management, personnel, purchasing, and receiving and materials handling). While these six departments do not constitute an entire hospital, the opportunities for improvement of management practices are abundant within them. Additionally, these six departments can be audited by an auditor who does not have a medical background. Any qualified auditor should be able to walk into a hospital and perform an operations audit by following the steps in the model (summarized below) and by utilizing the accompanying questionnaires (shown in Appendixes A through F) to interview hospital employees.

Procedural Review

The procedure for conducting an operations audit according to the model is reviewed here to provide a summary guide for the operations auditor who may wish to carry such an outline of the program with him during an audit.

1. The auditor should begin the audit with a physical walking tour (in the company of the controller or administrator) of the six departments being audited. The auditor's physical tour questions listed in Chapter 4 should be filled out either during or immediately following the tour. The auditor should make an effort to have a thorough enough knowledge of the questions so that it will not be necessary to refer to the list during the tour.

2. The auditor should acquire the following written data:

Written Goals and Objectives;
Policies and Procedures Manuals;
Job Descriptions;
Organization Chart;
Budgets;
Internal reports (prepared by each department of the business office);
Financial Statements;
HAS Reports;
Flow Charts;

Forms Used (by each department of the business office);
Minutes of the Board of Directors' Meetings.

3. The auditor should interview managerial level personnel and ask the preliminary-stage management questions listed in Chapter 4. The auditor should attempt to interview as many of the following individuals as possible:

Administrator;
Controller;
Admitting and Discharge Supervisor;
Payroll Supervisor;
Accounting Supervisor;
Purchasing Agent;
Receiving Supervisor;
Personnel Director.

4. The auditor should analyze the HAS Reports and compare the performance of the hospital being audited with the state averages for the same bed-size group. The list of ratios that would be significant to the operations auditor appears in Chapter 4.
5. The auditor should prepare a survey memorandum that isolates one or more departments for further study.
6. The auditor should perform the in-depth audit by utilizing one or more of the questionnaires illustrated in Appendixes A through F in interviews with all employees working in the department(s) selected for audit.
7. The auditor should prepare an audit report that lists possible problem areas.
8. The auditor should discuss the rough draft of the audit report with the head of the department that was audited in depth and, if necessary, revise the audit report prior to rendering the final copy.
9. The auditor should deliver the audit report both to top management and to the head of the department that was audited.

Recommendations for Further Study

As indicated earlier, many hospitals do have operating problems when compared to other hospitals and other businesses, and operations auditing, which has been almost nonexistent in hospitals, is designed to point out these problems. The model developed here—along with its accompanying questionnaires—simplifies the procedure and should thus help promulgate the benefits of operations audits for both auditors and auditees. However, since no other operations audit models for hospitals are known at this time, there is no way to determine whether this is the best possible model. It has been used as a guide in two hospital operations audits (see Appendix G for the results) and proved to be very workable and effective. For the future, its ability to simplify operations audits should prove equally effective for other hospitals and auditors since its format is easily adaptable to various types of departmentalized hospital business operations.

There are many other areas for potential research in the area of hospital business operations. For too long hospitals have been viewed as charitable institutions rather than as business entities. Hospitals must cover their costs in the same manner as any other institution. For that reason, any research that would treat hospitals as profit-seeking ventures would probably be beneficial. One particular topic that is recommended is research in the area of developing methods of measuring the efficiency of hospital operations.

In addition, there is still the question of who is best qualified to perform an operations audit. This research was conducted under the assumption that CPA firms would perform the operations audits for small hospitals. Research is needed, however, to determine at what point in size it would become more economical for the hospital to hire an internal operations auditor.

Appendixes

Appendix A: Operations Audit Questionnaire: Patient Census Management Department

Note: In a preliminary survey, six departmental managers in 84 hospitals were asked to rate the importance of each question listed below as follows: 0 = Not Important; 1 = Of Minor Importance; 2 = Important; and 3 = Very Important. The percentage of respondents who replied according to these scale rankings are shown in parentheses following each question; the figures in brackets represent the mean importance score for the question. A mean score of 1.0 or more was the criteria for selecting questions for the final questionnaire to be administered to departmental employees in the operations audit model.

Formal Policies and Procedures:

1. Have formal admissions policies and procedures been developed? (0 = –; 1 = –; 2 = 17%; 3 = 83% [2.829 mean])
2. Have formal discharge policies and procedures been developed? (0 = –; 1 = 0; 2 = 18%; 3 = 82% [2.824 mean])
3. Are all formal policies and procedures followed? (0 = –; 1 = 3%; 2 = 40%; 3 = 57% [2.543 mean])
4. Are all formal policies and procedures necessary; (0 = –; 1 = 3%; 2 = 35%; 3 = 62% [2.588 mean])

Financial Considerations:

5. Do you have a written financial policy to give or tell patients? (0 = –; 1 = –; 2 = 20%; 3 = 80% [2.8 mean])
6. Are patients ever asked for a financial statement prior to admission? (0 = 9%; 1 = 23%; 2 = 37%; 3 = 31% [1.914 mean])
7. Do you try and collect any part of a bill prior to admission when there is no third-party payor (or when bill will only be partially covered by third-party payor)? (0 = –; 1 = 6%; 2 = 32%; 3 = 62% [2.486 mean])
8. Has the feasibility of accepting charge cards (Master Charge, Bank Americard) been examined? (0 = 12%; 1 = 24%; 2 = 48%; 3 = 16% [1.667 mean])
9. Has factoring of receivables (or other bank payment plans) been considered? (0 = 6%; 1 = 25%; 2 = 60%; 3 = 9% [1.719 mean])
10. Does a regular policy exist for the use of a collection agency? (0 = 3%; 1 = 6%; 2 = 34%; 3 = 57% [2.457 mean])
    10-A. Is the efficiency of the collection agency ever determined? (0 = –; 1 = 3%; 2 = 30%; 3 = 67% [2.633 mean])

11. Are steps taken to find third-party payors for indigent patients? (0 = 3; 1 = –; 2 = 38%; 3 = 59% [2.529 mean])
12. What is the bad debt write-off percentage? (0 = –; 1 = 6%; 2 = 39%; 3 = 55% [2.484 mean])
13. Are departmental personnel knowledgeable enough to read and understand insurance policies? (0 = –; 1 = 3%; 2 = 24%; 3 = 73% [2.706 mean])
14. Are insurance policies verified at time of admission? (0 = –; 1 = –; 2 = 43%; 3 = 57% [2.571 mean])
15. Are steps taken to determine that all charges that should be made to a patient's account are made prior to the patient's discharge? (0 = –; 1 = 8%; 2 = 46%; 3 = 46% [2.371 mean])

Census Management:

16. Are patients treated with warmth and courtesy? (0 = –; 1 = –; 2 = 9%; 3 = 91% [2.914 mean])
17. Is the current census known at all times? (0 = 3%; 1 = 3%; 2 = 29%; 3 = 65% [2.571 mean])
18. How long do patients have to wait in the waiting room before being admitted? (0 = –; 1 = 3%; 2 = 32%; 3 = 65% [2.629 mean])
19. Are all admissions made by the admissions office? (0 = 3%; 1 = 6%; 2 = 40%; 3 = 51% [2.4 mean])
20. Is admissions office notified before any patient is put to bed? (0 = –; 1 = 6%; 2 = 23%; 3 = 71% [2.657 mean])
21. Are efforts made to stagger the time when new patients come in? (0 = 3%; 1 = 17%; 2 = 34%; 3 = 46% [2.229 mean])
22. Is there a system of priorities for admission? (0 = –; 1 = 9%; 2 = 24%; 3 = 67% [2.588 mean])
23. What is the percentage of pre-admissions to total admissions? (0 = –; 1 = 21%; 2 = 44%; 3 = 35% [2.147 mean])
24. Is pre-admission ever handled by mailing the forms to elective patients? (0 = 9%; 1 = 29%; 2 = 26%; 3 = 36% [1.914 mean])
25. Do you have a pre-admission diagnosis? (0 = 3%; 1 = 6%; 2 = 17%; 3 = 74% [2.629 mean])
26. Is doctor asked at pre-admission when patient will be discharged? (0 = 11%; 1 = 43%; 2 = 29%; 3 = 17% [1.514 mean])
27. Do admission forms contain spaces for all needed information? (0 = –; 1 = –; 2 = 17%; 3 = 83% [2.829 mean])
28. Do admission forms have spaces for only that information which is needed? (0 = 6%; 1 = 6%; 2 = 37%; 3 = 51% [2.343 mean])
29. Do you look at the surgical schedule in order to assign room types or plan for room changes? (0 = 9%; 1 = 17%; 2 = 25%; 3 = 49% [2.143 mean])
30. Are doctors made aware of the approach of maximum capacity? (0 = –; 1 = 6%; 2 = 38%; 3 = 56% [2.5 mean])

31. Are efforts made to find patients who can be dismissed early when 100% capacity is reached? (0 = —; 1 = 6%; 2 = 37%; 3 = 57% [2.514 mean])
32. Do you negotiate with doctors who want to admit patients at times of full capacity? (0 = 3%; 1 = 3%; 2 = 34%; 3 = 60% [2.514 mean])
33. Do you have emergency bed control by moving patients around to different parts of the hospital? (0 = —; 1 = 3%; 2 = 43%; 3 = 54% [2.514 mean])
34. Are doctors notified when vacant beds exist? (0 = 3%; 1 = 40%; 2 = 40%; 3 = 17% [1.714 mean])
35. Are doctors discouraged from admitting pseudo-emergencies? (0 = 3%; 1 = 19%; 2 = 44%; 3 = 34% [2.094 mean])
36. Are efforts made to maintain a profitable patient mix? (0 = 9%; 1 = 21%; 2 = 35%; 3 = 35% [1.938 mean])
37. Is the availability of beds and services at another institution checked prior to discharging a patient that is being transferred to that institution? (0 = 3%; 1 = 11%; 2 = 43%; 3 = 43% [2.257 mean])
38. Are any types of mathematical models used to fulfill the duties of the department (for example, queing theory)? (0 = 14%; 1 = 28%; 2 = 51%; 3 = 7% [1.517 mean])

Physical Facilities:

39. Does office layout lend itself to the normal flow of operations? (0 = —; 1 = —; 2 = 37%; 3 = 63% [2.629 mean])
40. Are physical conditions (smell, heat, etc.) of the department satisfactory? (0 = —; 1 = —; 2 = 43%; 3 = 57% [2.571 mean])
41. Is lighting adequate? (0 = —; 1 = —; 2 = 29%; 3 = 71% [2.714 mean])
42. Does the proper amount of floor space exist in the department? (0 = —; 1 = 3%; 2 = 34%; 3 = 63% [2.6 mean])
43. Are aisles wide enough for traffic? (0 = —; 1 = 6%; 2 = 37%; 3 = 57% [2.514 mean])
44. Is there ample waiting room space in or near the office?
45. Does each admitting and discharge officer have a private office? (0 = —; 1 = —; 2 = 46%; 3 = 54% [2.543 mean])
46. Are sufficient machines and equipment available? (0 = —; 1 = —; 2 = 26%; 3 = 74% [2.743 mean])
47. Are machines being used to maximum capacity? (0 = —; 1 = 15%; 2 = 35%; 3 = 50% [2.353 mean]
   47-A. If not, would sharing of machines be feasible? (0 = 4%; 1 = 17%; 2 = 50%; 3 = 29% [2.042 mean])
48. Is there any control over copying machine use? (0 = 3%; 1 = 21%; 2 = 47%; 3 = 29% [2.029 mean])
49. Are long distance phone calls approved by anyone? (0 = —; 1 = 24%; 2 = 44%; 3 = 32% [2.088 mean])
50. Is a record of reasons for long distance calls kept? (0 = 3%; 1 = 18%; 2 = 38%; 3 = 41% [2.177 mean])

Budgets:

51. Does the department prepare an annual expense budget? (0 = —; 1 = 9%; 2 = 29%; 3 = 62% [2.529 mean])
52. Is budget approved by anyone? (0 = —; 1 = 6%; 2 = 38%; 3 = 56% [2.5 mean])
53. Are budgets modified when conditions change? (0 = —; 1 = 9%; 2 = 47%; 3 = 44% [2.353 mean])
54. Are regular reports showing variances received? (0 = —; 1 = 9%; 2 = 42%; 3 = 49% [2.394 mean])
    54-A. Are significant variances from budget explained? (0 = —; 1 = 3%; 2 = 44%; 3 = 53% [2.5 mean])
55. Is a budget of daily census figures prepared? (0 = —; 1 = 9%; 2 = 47%; 3 = 44% [2.353 mean])
    55-A. Is the census budget prepared yearly? (0 = —; 1 = 12%; 2 = 36%; 3 = 52% [2.394 mean])
    55-B. Is the census budget prepared or updated monthly? (0 = 3%; 1 = 16%; 2 = 38%; 3 = 43% [2.219 mean])
    55-C. Are local doctors made aware of the budget? (0 = 3%; 1 = 18%; 2 = 33%; 3 = 46% [1.875 mean])
    55-D. Are occupancy goals set? (0 = 3%; 1 = 18%; 2 = 33%; 3 = 46% [2.212 mean])
    55-E. Are employees made aware of occupancy goals? (0 = 3%; 1 = 24%; 2 = 27%; 3 = 46% [2.152 mean])
    55-F. Is performance against the census budget assessed? (0 = —; 1 = 14%; 2 = 45%; 3 = 41% [2.276 mean])

Communications:

56. Is the communication between your department and other departments satisfactory? (0 = —; 1 = —; 2 = 14%; 3 = 86% [2.857 mean])
57. Do you feel you are provided with all information you need to fulfill your responsibilities? (0 = —; 1 = —; 2 = 17%; 3 = 83% [2.829 mean])
58. Do you receive any information or reports that you do not need? (0 = 6%; 1 = 19%; 2 = 44%; 3 = 31% [2.0 mean])
59. Do you process or analyze reports further in order to obtain needed information? (0 = —; 1 = 12%; 2 = 46%; 3 = 42% [2.303 mean])
60. Do you feel that all sections of the hospital business office have a good public relations image? (0 = —; 1 = —; 2 = 20%; 3 = 80% [2.857 mean])

Personnel:

61. Are job descriptions available for each position? (0 = —; 1 = —; 2 = 26%; 3 = 74% [2.735 mean])

62. Do you feel that everyone in your department has a thorough understanding of their job? (0 = —; 1 = —; 2 = 26%; 3 = 74% [2.735 mean])
63. What is the employee turnover rate? (0 = 3%; 1 = 6%; 2 = 50%; 3 = 41% [2.294 mean]
64. What is the employee absence rate? (0 = 3%; 1 = 3%; 2 = 32%; 3 = 62% [2.529 mean])
65. How many manhours are worked per admission? (0 = —; 1 = 6%; 2 = 50%; 3 = 44% [2.382 mean])
66. Is there a chain of supervision that goes into effect when absence or termination occurs? (0 = —; 1 = 11%; 2 = 37%; 3 = 52% [2.4 mean])
67. Are employees in view of supervision? (0 = —; 1 = 11%; 2 = 52%; 3 = 57% [2.257 mean])
68. Are efforts made to see that the department does not always operate at full capacity regardless of patient level? (0 = —; 1 = 28%; 2 = 41%; 3 = 31% [2.031 mean])
69. Does staff in department float to another department when work is excessive elsewhere? (0 = 9%; 1 = 12%; 2 = 56%; 3 = 23% [1.941 mean])
   69-A. Would such floating be feasible? (0 = 6%; 1 = 16%; 2 = 58%; 3 = 20% [1.903 mean])
70. Do employees in other departments float to this department when work is excessive in this department? (0 = 15%; 1 = 21%; 2 = 41%; 3 = 23% [1.735 mean])
   70-A. If not, would such floating be feasible? (0 = 14%; 1 = 21%; 2 = 41%; 3 = 24% [1.759 mean])
71. Are temporary employees ever used? (0 = 6%; 1 = 32%; 2 = 30%; 3 = 32% [1.882 mean])
72. Is overtime used to any great extent? (0 = 6%; 1 = 24%; 2 = 30%; 3 = 40% [2.059 mean])
73. Are future manpower needs forecast in order to minimize emergency recruitment? (0 = —; 1 = 3%; 2 = 47%; 3 = 50% [2.471 mean])
74. Is there any difficulty in obtaining approval to hire new employees? (0 = 3%; 1 = 9%; 2 = 50%, 3 = 38% [2.235 mean])
75. Is the number of staff and scheduling of staff commensurate with the department work load? (0 = —; 1 = —; 2 = 41%; 3 = 59% [2.588 mean])
76. Are employees encouraged to engage in some form of continuing education? (0 = —; 1 = 9%; 2 = 50%; 3 = 41% [2.324 mean])
77. Are employees encouraged to join professional organizations? (0 = 3%; 1 = 47%; 2 = 29%; 3 = 21% [1.677 mean])
78. Do personnel ever meet together as a group to discuss common problems? (0 = —; 1 = 11%; 2 ,34%; 3 = 55% [2.429 mean])
79. Does a suggestion box exist? (0 = 9%; 1 = 14%; 2 = 37%; 3 = 40% [2.086 mean])
   79-A. Are suggestions reviewed? (0 = 3%; 1 = 6%; 2 = 41%; 3 = 50% [2.375 mean])

79-B. Are accepted suggestions rewarded? (0 = 6%; 1 = 10%; 2 = 45%; 3 = 39% [2.161 mean])
80. Do you feel that all employees are loyal to the department and to the hospital? (0 = —; 1 = 3%; 2 = 31%; 3 = 66% [2.629 mean])

Appendix B:
Operations Audit Questionnaire:
Personnel Department

Note: In a preliminary survey, six departmental managers in 84 hospitals were asked to rate the importance of each question listed below as follows: 0 = Not Important; 1 = Of Minor Importance; 2 = Important; and 3 = Very Important. The percentage of respondents who replied according to these scale rankings are shown in parentheses following each question; the figures in brackets represent the mean importance score for the question. A mean score of 1.0 or more was the criteria for selecting questions for the final questionnaire to be administered to departmental employees in the operations audit model.

General:

1. Is there a centralized personnel function through which all applicants must pass? (0 = 5%; 1 = 2%; 2 = 23%; 3 = 70% [2.581 mean])
2. Is personnel a separate department from payroll? (0 = 19%; 1 = 28%; 2 = 23%; 3 = 30% [1.651 mean])
3. Is. the personnel department a "staff" function as opposed to a "line" function? (0 = 17%; 1 = 14%; 2 = 33%; 3 = 46% [2.186 mean])
4. Does personnel department have definite goals and objectives? (0 = 2%; 1 = 2%; 2 = 28%; 3 = 68% [2.605 mean])
5. Do the goals and objectives of the personnel department lead to the fulfillment of the goals and objectives of the hospital? (0 = 5%; 1 = 5%; 2 = 26%; 3 = 64% [2.512 mean])
6. Do you feel that management officials rely on the advice of the personnel department in areas of personnel management? (0 = 2%; 1 = 5%; 2 = 40%; 3 = 53% [2.429 mean])
7. Is the personnel department always involved in management decisions affecting employees? (0 = 5%; 1 = 7%; 2 = 33%; 3 = 55% [2.395 mean])
8. Does a procedures manual exist with written procedures and objectives for every job performed within the department? (0 = –; 1 = 2%; 2 = 37%; 3 = 61% [2.581 mean])
9. Is there an up-to-date published statement of personnel policies and procedures available to all hospital employees? (0 = –; 1 = –; 2 = 12%; 3 = 88% [2.884 mean])
10. Are personnel policies as set forth in the employee handbook honestly and uniformly applied? (0 = 2%; 1 = 5%; 2 = 19%; 3 = 74% [2.651 mean])
11. Are personnel policies written clearly so as to minimize the need for individual interpretation? (0 = 2%; 1 = 2%; 2 = 22%; 3 = 74% [2.674 mean])

12. Are personnel policies ever reviewed? (0 = —; 1 = 2%; 2 = 35%; 3 = 63% [2.605 mean])
13. Are job descriptions available for every position in the hospital? (0 = 27%; 1 = —; 2 = 37%; 3 = 61% [2.558 mean])
14. Is there a formal employee evaluation program? (0 = —; 1 = 12%; 2 = 30%; 3 = 58% [2.465 mean])
15. Do you know your costs for employee turnover and absenteeism? (0 = 5%; 1 = 12%; 2 = 58%; 3 = 25% [2.047 mean])
16. Are all aspects of personnel actions being processed done so in a timely and accurate manner? (0 = —; 1 = 9%; 2 = 56%; 3 = 35% [2.256 mean])
17. Is the final responsibility to hire and fire held by one person? (0 = 12%; 1 = 9%; 2 = 35%; 3 = 44% [2.116 mean])
18. Are all job applicants treated with consideration and courtesy? (0 = 2%; 1 = 5%; 2 = 24%; 3 = 69% [2.595 mean])
19. Is there an established wage and salary program to insure equitable rates of pay? (0 = —; 1 = —; 2 = 19%; 3 = 81% [2.814 mean])
20. Do you feel the pay system is truly a merit system? (0 = 2%; 1 = 9%; 2 = 49%; 3 = 40% [2.256 mean])
21. Is your fringe benefit program ever compared to those of businesses and hospitals in surrounding communities? (0 = —; 1 = 5%; 2 = 53%; 3 = 42% [2.372 mean])
22. Do you have a prescribed format for accepting and screening applicants? (0 = —; 1 = 21%; 2 = 47%; 3 = 32% [2.116 mean])
23. Does the department utilize a standard evaluation measure for screening applicants? (0 = 5%; 1 = 19%; 2 = 50%; 3 = 26% [1.976 mean])
24. Is the position control system based upon or correlated to the annual hospital budget? (0 = —; 1 = 12%; 2 = 46%; 3 = 42% [2.293 mean])
25. Do you feel the personnel department has a role that is well accepted by hospital management? (0 = 2%; 1 = 9%; 2 = 33%; 3 = 56% [2.419 mean])
26. Is there a staff planning program? (0 = 7%; 1 = 29%; 2 = 35%; 3 = 29% [1.857 mean])
27. Are future manpower needs forecast well enough to minimize emergency recruiting? (0 = 7%; 1 = 21%; 2 = 49%; 3 = 23% [1.884 mean])
28. Are benefit programs up to date? (0 = 2%; 1 = —; 2 = 51%; 3 = 47% [2.419 mean])
29. Are turnover statistics available for every position within the hospital? (0 = 9%; 1 = 26%; 2 = 49%; 3 = 16% [1.721 mean])
30. What is the average length of time a vacancy remains open? (0 = 5%; 1 = 40%; 2 = 35%; 3 = 20% [1.721 mean])
31. Is there an established grievance procedure? (0 = —; 1 = 5%; 2 = 26%; 3 = 69% [2.651 mean])
32. Is continuing education encouraged? (0 = 2%; 1 = 2%; 2 = 47%; 3 = 49% [2.419 mean])

33. Is there any type of employee development program? (0 = 2%; 1 = 21%; 2 = 45%; 3 = 32% [2.070])
34. Does there appear to be a reserve of trained talent for key executive replacement? (0 = 7%; 1 = 28%; 2 = 53%; 3 = 12% [1.700 mean])
35. Is an effort made to fill openings from within the hospital before recruiting outsiders? (0 = —; 1 = —; 2 = 47%; 3 = 53% [2.535 mean])
36. Is the performance of department heads appraised regularly? (0 = 2%; 1 = 9%; 2 = 30%; 3 = 59% [2.442 mean])
37. Do you try to minimize the length of time that a vacant position is left open? (0 = 7%; 1 = 12%; 2 = 47%; 3 = 34% [2.093 mean])
38. Are pre-employment physical examinations given? (0 = 2%; 1 = 14%; 2 = 44%; 3 = 40% [2.209 mean])
39. Is any personnel research being performed? (0 = 9%; 1 = 31%; 2 = 36%; 3 = 24% [1.738 mean])

Clerical Operations:

40. Are complete records kept on each employee? (0 = —; 1 = —; 2 = 14%; 3 = 86% [2.860 mean])
41. Do the departmental records meet the record keeping requirements of governmental agencies? (0 = 5%; 1 = 7%; 2 = 14%; 3 = 74% [2.581 mean])
42. Do record keeping and personnel forms contain spaces for all necessary information? (0 = 2%; 1 = 10%; 2 = 44%; 3 = 44% [2.302 mean])
43. Is all information on record keeping and personnel forms necessary? (0 = 5%; 1 = 14%; 2 = 60%; 3 = 21% [1.976 mean])
44. Are forms sizes convenient for filing? (0 = 7%; 1 = 26%; 2 = 43%; 3 = 24% [1.833 mean])
45. Is spacing on forms correct for easy typing? (0 = 9%; 1 = 29%; 2 = 50%; 3 = 12% [1.643 mean])
46. Is all filing of records kept up to date? (0 = 2%; 1 = 7%; 2 = 40%; 3 = 51% [2.395 mean])
47. Is the filing system easy to understand? (0 = 5%; 1 = 12%; 2 = 47%; 3 = 36% [2.163 mean])
48. Is there a system for immediately determining what positions are vacant? (0 = 2%; 1 = 14%; 2 = 42%; 3 = 42% [2.233 mean])
49. Are your position records such that any employee can be located at any time? (0 = —; 1 = 7%; 2 = 51%; 3 = 42% [2.349 mean])
50. Is there a system for updating information in personnel folders? (0 = 2%; 1 = 7%; 2 = 49%; 3 = 42% [2.302 mean])
51. Is there an adequate system for recording the promotion or transfer of hospital employees? (0 = 2%; 1 = 5%; 2 = 51%; 3 = 42% [2.326 mean])
52. Is there a system for immediate notification of the personnel department when an employee is terminated? (0 = —; 1 = —; 2 = 26%; 3 = 74% [2.744 mean])

53. Are references of potential employees thoroughly checked before applicants are hired? (0 = —; 1 = 2%; 2 = 26%; 3 = 72% [2.698 mean])

Departmental Staff:

54. Is there a job description for the director of personnel? (0 = 2%; 1 = 7%; 2 = 40%; 3 = 51% [2.395 mean])
55. Are all departmental employees knowledgeable about personnel policies and employee benefits? (0 = —; 1 = —; 2 = 26%; 3 = 74% [2.744 mean])
56. Do you feel all employees in the department are well qualified for their job? (0 = 5%; 1 = 5%; 2 = 39%; 3 = 51% [2.381 mean])
57. Are departmental employees knowledgeable about social security rules and regulations? (0 = 5%; 1 = 16%; 2 = 63%; 3 = 16% [1.970 mean])
58. Are all hirings made in compliance with EEO guidelines? (0 = —; 1 = 9%; 2 = 21%; 3 = 70% [2.605 mean])
59. Do you feel departmental employees are informed about labor laws? (0 = —; 1 = 12%; 2 = 56%; 3 = 32% [2.209 mean])
60. Is departmental staffing tailored to the workload? (0 = 5%; 1 = —; 2 = 51%; 3 = 44% [2.349 mean])
61. Has work been evenly distributed so that all employees within the department work steadily and efficiently? (0 = 5%; 1 = 2%; 2 = 42%; 3 = 51% [2.395 mean])
62. Is there an established line of authority within the department so that work goes on as usual when illness or termination occurs? (0 = 5%; 1 = 2%; 2 = 30%; 3 = 63% [2.512 mean])
63. What is the employee turnover rate within the department? (0 = 9%; 1 = 7%; 2 = 67%; 3 = 17% [1.907 mean])
64. What is the employee turnover rate for the entire hospital? (0 = 5%; 1 = 5%; 2 = 65%; 3 = 25% [2.116 mean])

Physical Facilities:

65. Are the physical facilities of the department adequate? (0 = 5%; 1 = —; 2 = 60%; 3 = 35% [2.259 mean])
66. Does the layout of the office lend itself to the normal flow of work? (0 = 5%; 1 = —; 2 = 72%; 3 = 23% [2.140 mean])
67. Do interviewers have their own private offices? (0 = 2%; 1 = 19%; 2 = 19%; 3 = 60% [2.372 mean])
68. Is the department easy to reach by the public? (0 = —; 1 = 12%; 2 = 39%; 3 = 49% [2.372 mean])
69. Is the department easy to reach by employees? (0 = —; 1 = 14%; 2 = 37%; 3 = 49% [2.349 mean])
70. Do you have sufficient equipment within the department? (0 = 5%; 1 = 14%; 2 = 53%; 3 = 28% [2.047 mean])

71. Is your budget for supplies and equipment large enough? (0 = 5%; 1 = 19%; 2 = 47%; 3 = 29% [2.023 mean])
72. Do you feel your total departmental budget is large enough? (0 = 5%; 1 = 14%; 2 = 58%; 3 = 23% [2.000 mean])
73. Do you feel you could operate just as efficiently on a smaller budget? (0 = 7%; 1 = 16%; 2 = 56%; 3 = 21% [1.907 mean])
74. Do you have an excessive amount of equipment in your department? (0 = 12%; 1 = 37%; 2 = 33%; 3 = 18% [1.581 mean])
75. Is there any control put upon copying machine use? (0 = 9%; 1 = 44%; 2 = 33%; 3 = 14% [1.512 mean])
76. Is a record kept of the reason for long distance phone calls? (0 = 5%; 1 = 28%; 2 = 49%; 3 = 18% [1.814 mean])

Communication:

77. Do you feel hospital employees understand the personnel policies? (0 = 2%; 1 = —; 2 = 12%; 3 = 86% [2.814 mean])
78. Are surveys ever made of employee feelings and impressions? (0 = —; 1 = 14%; 2 = 56%; 3 = 30% [2.163 mean])
79. Do hospital employees consider the personnel department as a "total information center?" (0 = 2%; 1 = 10%; 2 = 45%; 3 = 43% [2.286 mean])
80. Is there close coordination with the payroll department? (0 = —; 1 = 2%; 2 = 42%; 3 = 56% [2.535 mean])
81. Does the department have an open line of communication with all department heads and managers? (0 = —; 1 = —; 2 = 26%; 3 = 74% [2.744 mean])
82. Does the personnel department maintain an open door policy to all employees? (0 = 2%; 1 = 2%; 2 = 23%; 3 = 73% [2.651 mean])
83. Do employees feel free to come to the personnel department with their problems? (0 = —; 1 = 2%; 2 = 30%; 3 = 68% [2.651 mean])
84. Does a formal orientation program for new employees exist? (0 = —; 1 = 5%; 2 = 28%; 3 = 67% [2.628 mean])
85. Is there an internal newspaper or magazine for hospital employees? (0 = 16%; 1 = 16%; 2 = 44%; 3 = 24% [1.744 mean])
86. Is there a bulletin board available for communication of information to hospital employees? (0 = —; 1 = 5%; 2 = 56%; 3 = 39% [2.349 mean])
87. Does the hospital have a suggestion box? (0 = 14%; 1 = 28%; 2 = 47%; 3 = 11% [1.558 mean])
    87-A. Are accepted suggestions rewarded? (0 = 8%; 1 = 27%; 2 = 51%; 3 = 14% [1.703 mean])
88. Are future supervisors of new employees brought into the hiring process? (0 = 5%; 1 = 12%; 2 = 47%; 3 = 36% [2.163 mean])
89. Is a nondiscrimination policy clearly stated and posted? (0 = —; 1 = 5%; 2 = 21%; 3 = 74% [2.698 mean])
90. Are all reports you receive timely and informative? (0 = 2%; 1 = 5%; 2 = 51%; 3 = 42% [2.326 mean])

91. Are all reports you prepare timely and informative to others? (0 = —; 1 = 7%; 2 = 49%; 3 = 44% [2.372 mean])

Appendix C: Operations Audit Questionnaire: Accounting Department

Note: In a preliminary survey, six departmental managers in 84 hospitals were asked to rate the importance of each question listed below as follows: 0 = Not Important; 1 = Of Minor Importance; 2 = Important; and 3 = Very Important. The percentage of respondents who replied according to these scale rankings are shown in parentheses following each question; the figures in brackets represent the mean importance score for the question. A mean score of 1.0 or more was the criteria for selecting questions for the final questionnaire to be administered to departmental employees in the operations audit model.

General:

1. Is there a procedures manual for the department? (0 = —; 1 = 8%; 2 = 20%; 3 = 72% [2.64 mean])
2. Have steps been taken to provide assurance that the established procedures are being followed? (0 = —; 1 = 8%; 2 = 20%; 3 = 72% [2.64 mean])
3. Are the reports that you prepare used by anyone? (0 = —; 1 = 4%; 2 = 40%; 3 = 56% [2.52 mean])
4. Is there a "How to Use" manual for the reports you prepare? (0 = 12%; 1 = 4%; 2 = 40%; 3 = 12% [1.52 mean])
5. Is there an organization chart defining where individuals in the department stand with each other and where the department stands in relation to the rest of the hospital? (0 = 4%; 1 = 16%; 2 = 40%; 3 = 40% [2.16 mean])
6. Is pertinent historical and projected financial data provided accurately, speedily, and in meaningful form? (0 = —; 1 = —; 2 = 16%; 3 = 84% [2.84 mean])
7. Is financial and statistical data sufficient for use as a means of performance evaluation and appraisal? (0 = —; 1 = 4%; 2 = 48%; 3 = 48% [2.44 mean])
8. Is the accrual system of accounting used (as opposed to a cash basis system)? (0 = 4%; 1 = 4%; 2 = 40%; 3 = 52% [2.4 mean])
9. Is there an open line of communication with all other departments? (0 = —; 1 = 12%; 2 = 36%; 3 = 52% [2.4 mean])
10. Is the accounting system complex and complete enough to give accurate cost figures for all items in each department? (0 = —; 1 = —; 2 = 40%; 3 = 60% [2.6 mean])
11. Are the books of account adequate for this size hospital? (0 = —; 1 = —; 2 = 32%; 3 = 68% [2.68 mean])

12. Is the equipment within the department adequate? (0 = —; 1 = —; 2 = 60%; 3 = 40% [2.4 mean])
13. Are the physical facilities of the office adequate? (0 = —; 1 = 12%; 2 = 60%; 3 = 28% [2.16 mean])
14. Is lighting sufficient? (0 = —; 1 = 12%; 2 = 56%; 3 = 32% [2.2 mean])
15. Does the hospital subscribe and contribute to HAS (Hospital Advisory Services, published by the American Hospital Association)? 0 = 4%; 1 = 24%; 2 = 60%; 3 = 12% [1.792 mean])
16. Are there ever audits of the department? (0 = —; 1 = —; 2 = 40%; 3 = 60% [2.6 mean])
17. How many days of revenue are in accounts receivable? (0 = —; 1 = 8%; 2 = 32%; 3 = 60% [2.52 mean])
18. What percentage is the allowance for bad debts of total accounts receivable? (0 = —; 1 = 12%; 2 = 28%; 3 = 60% [2.48 mean])

Budgets:

19. Has someone questioned whether the cost of developing the hospital budget is equal to its projected value? (0 = 8%; 1 = 36%; 2 = 36%; 3 = 20% [1.68 mean])
20. Are budgets the result of challenged calculations as opposed to figures developed without analysis from prior experience? (0 = —; 1 = 4%; 2 = 52%; 3 = 44% [2.4 mean])
21. Are budgets prepared by people responsible for meeting them? (0 = —; 1 = —; 2 = 32%; 3 = 68% [2.68 mean])
22. Do budgets include cushions or fat that would dilute the effectiveness of the control instrument? (0 = 4%; 1 = 13%; 2 = 33%; 3 = 50% [2.292 mean])
23. Are written budgets prepared for future changes in plans? (0 = —; 1 = 13%; 2 = 33%; 3 = 54% [2.417 mean])
24. Do you utilize cash flow budgets? (0 = —; 1 ,13%; 2 = 37%; 3 = 50% [2.375 mean])
25. Are cash flow budgets updated periodically? (0 = 8%; 1 = 8%; 2 = 50%; 3 = 42% [2.333 mean])
26. Is accounting aware of the budgets of all departments? (0 = —; 1 = 13%; 2 = 29%; 3 = 58% [2.458 mean])
27. Are actual-versus-budget reports prepared? (0 = —; 1 = —; 2 = 33%; 3 = 67% [2.667 mean])
28. Is the accounting department budget adequate? (0 = —; 1 = 13%; 2 = 42%; 3 = 45% [2.333 mean])

Internal Control:

29. Is there a written internal control policy? (0 = 4%; 1 = 8%; 2 = 30%; 3 = 58% [2.417 mean])

30. Do you feel that there is a separation of duties among employees that provides for good internal control? (0 = —; 1 = 3%; 2 = 30%; 3 = 67% [2.625 mean])
31. Are journal entries supported by substantiating data? (0 = 4%; 1 = —; 2 = 21%; 3 = 75% [2.667 mean])
32. Are employees bonded? (0 = —; 1 = 17%; 2 = 33%; 3 = 50% [2.333 mean])
33. Are employees required to take vacations at least annually? (0 = —; 1 = 21%; 2 = 38%; 3 = 41% [2.208 mean])
34. Are duties periodically rotated among different employees? (0 = 4%; 1 = 33%; 2 = 50%; 3 = 13% [1.708 mean])
35. Are allowances for discounts to certain types of patients authorized by a responsible official? (0 = 4%; 1 = 8%; 2 = 33%; 3 = 55% [2.375 mean])
36. Is it hospital policy to require approval by a responsible official before an account may be written off as a bad debt? (0 = 4%; 1 = 4%; 2 = 29%; 3 = 63% [2.5 mean])
37. Is it hospital policy to have receipts deposited in the bank and recorded in the cash receipts journal daily? (0 = —; 1 = —; 2 = 13%; 3 = 87% [2.875 mean])
38. Are receipts deposited intact without making small payments in cash prior to going to the bank? (0 = —, 1 = 13%; 2 = 25%; 3 = 62% [2.5 mean])
39. Is it hospital policy to have vouchers and supporting documents presented simultaneously with checks for signature? (0 = —; 1 = 8%; 2 = 21%; 3 = 71% [2.625 mean])
40. Are vouchers and supporting invoices effectively canceled (marked paid) after related checks have been signed in order to prevent duplicate payment? (0 = —; 1 = —; 2 = 25%; 3 = 75% [2.75 mean])
41. Are checks prenumbered? (0 = —; 1 = 4%; 2 = 21%; 3 = 75% [2.708 mean])
42. Is a check protector used? (0 = 4%; 1 = 13%; 2 = 29%; 3 = 54% [2.333 mean])
43. Are checks signed by someone other than the preparer? (0 = —; 1 = 8%; 2 = 17%; 3 = 75% [2.667 mean])
44. Are individuals who are authorized to sign checks limited to employees who have no access to accounting records, cash receipts, or petty cash funds? (0 = 17%; 1 = 8%; 2 = 46%; 3 = 29% [1.875 mean])
45. Is the bank statement reconciled monthly? (0 = —; 1 = —; 2 = 4%; 3 = 96% [2.958 mean])
46. Does someone other than the preparer of checks perform the bank reconciliation? (0 = 8%; 1 = 30%; 2 = 38%; 3 = 54% [2.375 mean])
47. Are signed checks mailed without returning them to the individual who prepared them? (0 = 8%; 1 = 21%; 2 = 29%; 3 = 42% [2.042 mean])
48. Does the person who prepares the bank deposits also have anything to do with customers' ledgers? (0 = —; 1 = 17%; 2 = 29%; 3 = 54% [2.375 mean])
49. Have instructions been issued to the bank not to cash checks payable to the hospital and to accept them for deposit only? (0 = —; 1 = 4%; 2 = 21%; 3 = 75% [2.708 mean])

Procedures:

50. How long after the close of the month is it before financial reports are generated? (0 = 4%; 1 = 4%; 2 = 33%; 3 = 59% [2.458 mean])
51. Are financial statements prepared monthly? (0 = —; 1 = —; 2 = 21%; 3 = 79% [2.792 mean]
* Are financial statements published in the newspaper? (0 = 59%; 1 = 25%; 2 = 8%; 3 = 8% [.667 mean])
52. Are reports correct as issued or do they contain errors? (0 = —; 1 = —; 2 = 33%; 3 = 67% [2.667 mean])
53. Are there any bottlenecks in the paper flow? (0 = 4%; 1 = 4%; 2 = 46%; 3 = 46% [2.333 mean])
54. Are all tasks that are performed necessary? (0 = 4%; 1 = 13%; 2 = 50%; 3 = 33% [2.125 mean])
55. Has the possibility been examined of using a computer or timesharing of a computer? (0 = 4%; 1 = 13%; 2 = 46%; 3 = 33% [2.042 mean])
56. Are internal reports to management prepared in a manner to highlight unusual variations in figures? (0 = —; 1 = —; 2 = 25%; 3 = 75% [2.75 mean])
57. Have you examined the possibility of reducing posting time by doing more summary posting? (0 = —; 1 = 4%; 2 = 75%; 3 = 21% [2.167 mean])
58. Do you take advantage of all possible cash discounts? (0 = —; 1 = —; 2 = 21%; 3 = 79% [2.792 mean])
59. Does the accounting system show what amount of cash discounts are not taken (for example, is there a Discounts Lost account)? (0 = 21%; 1 = 25%; 2 = 38%; 3 = 16% [1.5 mean])
60. Are receivables totals compared to the control account balance at monthly intervals? (0 = —; 1 = —; 2 = 25%; 3 = 75% [2.75 mean])
61. Are errors ever uncovered when receivable and payable ledger totals are compared to the control account balances? (0 = —; 1 = —; 2 = 33%; 3 = 67% [2.667 mean])
62. Are there ledgers for items of property and equipment? (0 = —, 1 = —; 2 = 42%; 3 = 58% [2.583 mean])
63. Are property, plant, and equipment ledgers balanced periodically with general ledger control accounts? (0 = —; 1 = —; 2 = 38%; 3 = 62% [2.625 mean])
64. Is a periodic inventory of plant and equipment items taken? (0 = 4%; 1 = 4%; 2 = 34%; 3 = 58% [2.458 mean])
65. Is depreciation of plant and equipment recorded in the hospital accounts? (0 = 1; 1 = 4%; 2 = 25%; 3 = 71% [2.667 mean])
66. Are all revenues and expenses always posted to the proper departments? (0 = —; 1 = —; 2 = 17%; 3 = 83% [2.833 mean])

*This question did not meet the requirement for inclusion in the final questionnaire; it is shown here merely to provide a complete view of the preliminary survey instrument.

67. Do all charges get posted promptly to the proper patient accounts? (0 = —; 1 = —; 2 = 13%; 3 = 87% [2.875 mean])
68. Are insurance policy claims filed promptly and is there any follow-up if payment is delayed? (0 = —; 1 = —; 2 = 21%; 3 = 79% [2.792 mean])
69. Are accounts receivables aged regularly? (0 = —; 1 = 8%; 2 = 21%; 3 = 71% [2.625 mean])
70. Are statements mailed out regularly? (0 = —; 1 = —; 2 = 25%; 3 = 75% [2.833 mean])
71. Is the hospital price list kept up to date? (0 = —; 1 = —; 2 = 38; 3 = 62% [2.75 mean])
72. Is the size of checking account balances excessive in line with current cash needs? (0 = —; 1 = —; 2 = 38%; 3 = 62% [2.625 mean])
73. Is excess cash ever used for short-term investments? (0 = 4%; 1 = 8%; 2 = 25%; 3 = 63% [2.458 mean])
74. Is copying machine use controlled? (0 = 4%; 1 = 12%; 2 = 42%; 3 = 42% [2.208 mean])

Departmental Staff:

75. Is there a job description for every position within the department? (0 = 4%; 1 = —; 2 = 29%; 3 = 67% [2.583 mean])
76. Is there any type of employee orientation and training program or manual? (0 = —; 1 = 12%; 2 = 38%; 3 = 50% [2.375 mean])
77. Do you feel that all employees in the department take pride in their work? (0 = —; 1 = —; 2 = 58%; 3 = 42% [2.417 mean])
78. Do employees have a favorable attitude toward the department and the hospital? (0 = —; 1 = —; 2 = 46%; 3 = 54% [2.542 mean])
79. Are employees competent to perform the duties they are supposed to be performing? (0 = —; 1 = —; 2 = 33%; 3 = 67% [2.667 mean])
80. Do you feel that all employees in the department are loyal to the hospital? (0 = —; 1 = 4%; 2 = 46%; 3 = 50% [2.458 mean])
81. Do you feel that employees are knowledgeable in all areas of accounting and not just the small area in which they work? (0 = —; 1 = 13%; 2 = 54%; 3 = 33% [2.208 mean])
82. What is the employee turnover rate? (0 = —; 1 = 4%; 2 = 50%; 3 = 46% [2.417 mean])
83. What is the employee absence rate? (0 = —; 1 = —; 2 = 46%; 3 = 54% [2.542 mean])
84. Do all employees in the department have an education in accounting? (0 = —; 1 = 17%; 2 = 75%; 3 = 8% [1.917 mean])
85. Are accountants paid at approximately the same level as accountants in private industry and public accounting? (0 = 4%; 1 = 8%; 2 = 50%; 3 = 38% [2.208 mean])

86. Are there standards of performance for each position which measure in quantitative terms the accounting employees' performance? (0 = 8%; 1 = 8%; 2 = 50%; 3 = 34% [2.083 mean])
87. Does the accounting department ever work overtime for which a premium pay rate is received? (0 = —; 1 = 42%; 2 = 33%; 3 = 25% [1.833 mean])
88. Has the possibility been considered of hiring temporary employees to assist in performing the month end work? (0 = 17%; 1 = 46%; 2 = 17%; 3 = 20% [1.417 mean])
89. Is the workload arranged so that one person is not idle while another is overloaded? (0 = —; 1 = 4%; 2 = 54%; 3 = 22% [2.375 mean])
90. Do you feel any employees in the department are overburdened with work? (0 = —; 1 = 8%; 2 = 54%; 3 = 38% [2.292 mean])
91. Is continuing education encouraged? (0 = —; 1 = 4%; 2 = 46%; 3 = 50% [2.458 mean])
92. Is membership in professional organizations encouraged? (0 = 8%; 1 = 17%; 2 = 29%; 3 = 56% [2.125 mean])
93. Does the hospital have an internal auditor? (0 = —; 1 = 8%; 2 = 54%; 3 = 38% [2.292 mean])

Appendix D:
Operations Audit Questionnaire:
Payroll Department

Note: In a preliminary survey, six departmental managers in 84 hospitals were asked to rate the importance of each question listed below as follows: 0 =Not Important; 1 = Of Minor Importance; 2 = Important; and 3 = Very Important. The percentage of respondents who replied according to these scale rankings are shown in parentheses following each question; the figures in brackets represent the mean importance score for the question. A mean score of 1.0 or more was the criteria for selecting questions for the final questionnaire to be administered to departmental employees in the operations audit model.

Controls:

1. Are employee time cards used? (0 = 5%; 1 = 5%; 2 = 21%; 3 = 69% [2.538 mean])
2. Does anyone oversee the clocking in process? (0 = 26%; 1 = 29%; 2 = 26%; 3 = 19% [1.368 mean])
    2-A. Is the job of overseer rotated regularly? (0 = 38%; 1 = 24%; 2 = 31%; 3 = 7% [1.069 mean])
3. Is an employee's initial salary authorized in writing by someone qualified to do so? (0 = 3%; 1 = —; 2 = 10%; 3 = 87% [2.821 mean])
4. Are salary changes authorized in writing? (0 = 3%; 1 = —; 2 = 10%; 3 = 87% [2.821 mean])
5. Are time card or time sheet clerical calculations ever audited? (0 = —; 1 = 2%; 2 = 49%; 3 = 49% [2.462 mean])
6. Are firings or resignations reported to payroll in writing? (0 = —; 1 = 8%; 2 = 26%; 3 = 66% [2.590 mean])
7. Are all payroll department employees bonded? (0 = 19%; 1 = 25%; 2 = 28%; 3 = 28% [1.639 mean])
8. Are employees paid by check? (0 = —; 1 = 5%; 2 = 10%; 3 = 85% [2.795 mean])
9. Are checks prenumbered? (0 = 3%; 1 = 3%; 2 = 18%; 3 = 76% [2.692 mean])
10. Are checks signed by someone other than the preparer? (0 = 5%; 1 = 3%; 2 = 23%; 3 = 69% [2.564 mean])
11. Are checks kept locked up when not being used? (0 = 3%; 1 = —; 2 = 41%; 3 = 56% [2.513 mean])
12. Is a check protector used? (0 = 8%; 1 = 10%; 2 = 41%; 3 = 41% [2.154 mean])
13. Does someone other than those with access to the payroll checks reconcile

the bank account monthly? (0 = 8%; 1 = 24%; 2 = 18%; 3 = 50% [2.105 mean])
14. Does the reconciling of the bank account include checking for double endorsements on payroll checks? (0 = 26%; 1 = 28%; 2 = 31%; 3 = 15% [1.359 mean])
15. Are unclaimed paychecks handled in a special manner? (0 = 3%; 1 = 13%; 2 = 46%; 3 = 38% [2.205 mean])
16. Does a special procedure exist for issuing corrected checks when errors do occur? (0 = 5%; 1 = 8%; 2 = 41%; 3 = 46% [2.282 mean])
* Are the duties of payroll employees rotated regularly? (0 = 31%; 1 = 46%; 2 = 20%; 3 = 3% [.949 mean])
17. Are payroll employees required to take vacations at least annually? (0 = 23%; 1 = 20%; 2 = 31%; 3 = 26% [1.590 mean])
18. Are payroll checks distributed by someone other than the payroll employees and the head nurses? (0 = 23%; 1 = 26%; 2 = 33%; 3 = 18% [1.462 mean])
* Is the duty of distributing paychecks rotated regularly? (0 = 41%; 1 = 46%; 2 = 10%; 3 = 3% [.744 mean])
* Are special duty nurses paid in a different manner than regular nurses? (0 = 47%; 1 = 25%; 2 = 19%; 3 = 9% [.889 mean])
19. Is the special duty nurse payroll ever checked against the names of the employees on the regular payroll? (0 = 33%; 1 = 25%; 2 = 25%; 3 = 17% [1.250 mean])

Procedures:

20. Is payroll always completed on time? (0 = —; 1 = —; 2 = 23%; 3 = 77% [2.769 mean])
21. Do you receive all time cards and other payroll information prior to the time when they are needed? (0 = 5%; 1 = 3%; 2 = 23%; 3 = 69% [2.564 mean])
22. Are time cards kept long enough to meet legal requirements? (0 = —; 1 = 3%; 2 = 18%; 3 = 79% [2.769 mean])
23. Is a separate payroll bank account used? (0 = 3%; 1 = 13%; 2 = 23%; 3 = 61% [2.436 mean])
* Has the possibility of utilizing several special payroll accounts been examined? (0 = 38%; 1 = 38%; 2 = 21%; 3 = 3% [.872 mean])
* Has the possibility been examined of writing only one payroll check (payable to a bank) and letting the bank make out deposit slips for the individual employees? (0 = 46%; 1 = 36%; 2 = 15%; 3 = 3% [.000 mean])
24. Has the possibility of reducing the frequency of payroll been considered? (0 = 26%; 1 = 31%; 2 = 33%; 3 = 10% [1.282 mean])
25. Has the possibility of using a computer service center or a "one-write" system been examined? (0 = 10%; 1 = 10%; 2 = 44%; 3 = 36% [2.051 mean])
26. Are payroll figures reported by department? (0 = 13%; 1 = 3%; 2 = 31%; 3 = 53% [2.256 mean])

*These questions did not meet the requirement for inclusion in the final questionnaire; they are shown here merely to provide a complete view of the preliminary survey instrument.

27. Is a trend analysis ever made of gross payroll figures? (0 = 3%; 1 = 23%; 2 = 37%; 3 = 37% [2.079 mean])
* Are donated services recorded as expenses in the payroll accounts? (0 = 51%; 1 = 27%; 2 = 14%; 3 = 8% [.784 mean])
28. Are quarterly tax reports always filed on time? (0 = —; 1 = —; 2 = 8%; 3 = 92% [2.923 mean])
29. Are withholding tax deposits always made on time? (0 = —; 1 = —; 2 = 8%; 3 = 92% [2.923 mean])
30. Are quarterly reports always typed within a reasonable length of time after they have been prepared? (0 = —; 1 = 5%; 2 = 23%; 3 = 72% [2.667 mean])
31. Are problems that affect work discussed with the head nurses or other department heads of the area that is at fault? (0 = —; 1 = —; 2 = 38%; 3 = 62% [2.615 mean])
32. Does the payroll department operate without requiring any overtime work? (0 = 3%; 1 = 21%; 2 = 44%; 3 = 32% [2.077 mean])
  32-A. How much overtime is worked? (0 = 10%; 1 = 14%; 2 = 48%; 3 = 28% [1.931 mean])
33. Is overtime within the department authorized by anyone? (0 = —; 1 = —; 2 = 43%; 3 = 57% [2.568 mean])

Physical Facilities:

34. Are the physical facilities of the department adequate? (0 = —; 1 = 8%; 2 = 66%; 3 = 26% [2.179 mean])
35. Are an adequate number of office machines always available when you need them? (0 = —; 1 = 2%; 2 = 49%; 3 = 49% [2.462 mean])
36. Are additional office machines available from other departments if needed during extra busy periods? (0 = —; 1 = 24%; 2 = 45%; 3 = 31% [2.079 mean])
37. Is all equipment fully utilized? (0 = —; 1 = 13%; 2 = 56%; 3 = 31% [2.179 mean])
38. Would a lesser number of machines result in less efficiency? (0 = 3%; 1 = 22%; 2 = 56%; 3 = 19% [1.917 mean])
39. Is there a specified procedure to follow when the purchase of new machines is necessary? (0 = 5%; 1 = 8%; 2 = 34%; 3 = 53% [2.342 mean])
40. Is the department overstocked with supplies that it will either not use in the near future or will never use? (0 = 3%; 1 = 13%; 2 = 64%; 3 = 20% [2.026 mean])

Personnel:

41. Are the employees of the department well qualified to perform the duties that are required of them? (0 = —; 1 = —; 2 = 26%; 3 = 74% [2.744 mean])

---

*This question did not meet the requirement for inclusion in the final questionnaire; it is shown here merely to provide a complete view of the preliminary survey instrument.

42. Do you feel that all employees within the department keep the information that they come in contact with confidential? (0 = —; 1 = —; 2 =,18%; 3 = 82% [2.641 mean])
43. Do you feel the working atmosphere in the department is relaxed and one of openness? (0 = —; 1 = 3%; 2 = 58%; 3 = 39% [2.368 mean])
44. Is continuing education encouraged? (0 = 3%; 1 = 8%; 2 = 46%; 3 = 43% [2.308 mean])
45. Has work been evenly distributed so that all employees within the department work steadily and efficiently? (0 = —; 1 = —; 2 = 59%; 3 = 41% [2.410 mean])
46. Is the department adequately staffed? (0 = —; 1 = —; 2 = 48%; 3 = 52% [2.513 mean])
47. Have temporary employees been considered for performing end-of-the-quarter work? (0 = 21%; 1 = 38%; 2 = 28%; 3 = 13% [1.333 mean])
48. Is it a fairly easy process to hire new employees when they are needed? (0 = 5%; 1 = 23%; 2 = 56%; 3 = 16% [1.821 mean])
49. Do payroll department employees "float" to other departments during slack periods? (0 = 29%; 1 = 18%; 2 = 35%; 3 = 18% [1.421 mean])
   49-A. Would such floating be feasible? (0 = 36%; 1 = 21%; 2 = 29%; 3 = 14% [1.214 mean])
50. Do employees of other departments "float" to the payroll department during busy periods? (0 = 29%; 1 = 21%; 2 = 18%; 3 = 32% [1.526 mean])
   50-A. Would such floating be feasible? (0 = 38%; 1 = 17%; 2 = 14%; 3 = 31% [1.379 mean])
51. Are departmental employees familiar with the requirements of the Federal Wage and Hour laws? (0 = 3%; 1 = 10%; 2 = 26%; 3 = 61% [2.462 mean])
52. What is the employee turnover rate? (0 = 14%; 1 = 3%; 2 = 57%; 3 = 26% [1.973 mean])
53. What is the absenteeism rate? (0 = 11%; 1 = 5%; 2 = 53%; 3 = 31% [2.053 mean])
54. What is the ratio of payroll personnel to total employees? (0 = 16%; 1 = 19%; 2 = 39%; 3 = 26% [1.763 mean])

General:

55. Does a procedures manual exist with written procedures and objectives for every job performed within the department? (0 = —; 1 = 5%; 2 = 28%; 3 = 67% [2.395 mean])
56. Is there an open line of communication between the department and the individuals to whom the department head reports? (0 = —; 1 = 5%; 2 = 28%; 3 = 67% [2.615 mean])
57. Are payroll reports organized in such a way as to be useful management tools? (0 = 3%; 1 = —; 2 = 38%; 3 = 59% [2.538 mean])

58. Are job descriptions and areas of responsibility sufficiently defined in writing? (0 = —; 1 = 5%; 2 = 46%; 3 = 49% [2.436 mean])
59. Is any type of personnel budget utilized within the department? (0 = 5%; 1 = 13%; 2 = 46%; 3 = 36% [2.128 mean])
60. Is payroll advised of the payroll budget for each department so that there is an awareness of the allotted amount? (0 = 11%; 1 = 18%; 2 = 45%; 3 = 26% [1.868 mean])
61. Do the employee payroll records contain spaces for all information that needs to be recorded? (0 = —; 1 = 8%; 2 = 31%; 3 = 61% [2.538 mean])
62. Is all of the information in the payroll records needed? (0 = —; 1 = 10%; 2 = 44%; 3 = 46% [2.359 mean])
63. Is the hospital eligible for merit reductions in state unemployment taxes? (0 = 3%; 1 = 11%; 2 = 50%; 3 = 36% [2.211 mean])
64. Are the effects on merit reductions considered when layoffs appear likely? (0 = 5%; 1 = 22%; 2 = 48%; 3 = 25% [1.917 mean])
65. Is the hospital eligible for merit reductions in workman's compensation rates? (0 = 13%; 1 = 8%; 2 = 47%; 3 = 32% [1.974 mean])
66. Is the effect on the merit rating ever considered when minor injuries occur? (0 = 8%; 1 = 29%; 2 = 42%; 3 = 21% [1.763 mean])
67. How often are errors made in the preparation of payroll? (0 = —; 1 = 5%; 2 = 18%; 3 = 77% [2.718 mean])
68. What problems, if any, do you feel exist within the department? (0 = 3%; 1 = 3%; 2 = 50%; 3 = 44% [2.333 mean])

Appendix E: Operations Audit Questionnaire: Purchasing Department

Note: In a preliminary survey, six departmental managers in 84 hospitals were asked to rate the importance of each question listed below as follows: 0 = Not Important; 1 = Of Minor Importance; 2 = Important; and 3 = Very Important. The percentage of respondents who replied according to these scale rankings are shown in parentheses following each question; the figures in brackets represent the mean importance score for the question. A mean score of 1.0 or more was the criteria for selecting questions for the final questionnaire to be administered to departmental employees in the operations audit model.

General:

1. Does the hospital utilize a centralized purchasing system? (0 = —; 1 = —; 2 = 12%; 3 = 88% [2.88 mean])
2. Do you feel that other departments view the purchasing department as an information center for solving any type of material problems? (0 = —; 1 = 4%; 2 = 42%; 3 = 54% [2.5 mean])
3. Are purchase requests always executed on a timely basis? (0 = —; 1 = 4%; 2 = 29%; 3 = 67% [2.625 mean])
4. How often does an out-of-stock situation occur? (0 = —; 1 = 8%; 2 = 46%; 3 = 46% [2.375 mean])
5. Is overstocking a problem? (0 = —; 1 = 12%; 2 = 38%; 3 = 50% [2.375 mean])
6. Are purchase orders used for all buying? (0 = —; 1 = 4%; 2 = 29%; 3 = 67% [2.625 mean])
7. Is purchasing separate from the receiving function? (0 = 8%; 1 = 17%; 2 = 46%; 3 = 29% [1.958 mean])
8. Do you try and acquire generic products as opposed to brand name products? (0 = —; 1 = 21%; 2 = 62%; 3 = 17% [1.958 mean])
9. How much time is required to process a request for purchase? (0 = —; 1 = 8%; 2 = 71%; 3 = 21% [2.125 mean])
10. What is the cost (or manhours) per purchase order? (0 = 4%; 1 = 33%; 2 = 50%; 3 = 13% [1.708 mean])
11. Is there an adequate library of catalogs and current price list? (0 = —; 1 = —; 2 = 46%; 3 = 54% [2.542 mean])
12. Is there an inventory control system? (0 = —; 1 = 4%; 2 = 4%; 3 = 92% [2.875 mean])

13. Is the purchasing department "service" oriented? (0 = 4%; 1 = —; 2 = 42%; 3 = 54% [2.458 mean])
14. Do you have records of the amount of time that is spent talking to salesmen? (0 = 33%; 1 = 33%; 2 = 29%; 3 = 4% [1.042 mean])
15. Have dollar purchases and approval limits been established? (0 = —; 1 = 4%; 2 = 50%; 3 = 46% [2.417 mean])
16. Are purchases (both in dollars and number of orders) known for each department in the hospital? (0 = —; 1 = 8%; 2 = 71%; 3 = 21% [2.125 mean])
17. Is there a Product Evaluation Committee? (0 = 4%; 1 = —; 2 = 63%; 3 = 33% [2.25 mean])
    17-A. Is purchasing agent a member of the Committee? (0 = 4%; 1 = —; 2 = 46%; 3 = 50% [2.417 mean])
18. Does the purchasing department maintain an equipment ledger for capital equipment? (0 = 8%; 1 = 13%; 2 = 46%; 3 = 33% [2.042 mean])
19. Is copying machine use controlled? (0 = 4%; 1 = 21%; 2 = 50%; 3 = 25% [2.0 mean])
20. Are you aware of the amount invested in inventory at all times so that money is not tied up for excessive periods of time? (0 = —; 1 = —; 2 = 25%; 3 = 75 [2.75 mean])
21. Are price variances used as a measure of purchasing agent performance? (0 = —; 1 = 29%; 2 = 46%; 3 = 25% [1.958 mean])
22. Are there rules against conflict of interest such as ownership by purchasing agent of stock in suppliers? (0 = —; 1 = 21%; 2 = 42%; 3 = 37% [2.167 mean])
23. Are the physical facilities of the department adequate? (0 = —; 1 = 4%; 2 = 46%; 3 = 50% [2.458 mean])
24. Is an adequate amount of office equipment available in the department? (0 = —; 1 = 4%; 2 = 54%; 3 = 42% [2.375 mean])

Communication:

25. Does purchasing department have good relations with other departments? (0 = —; 1 = —; 2 = 21%; 3 = 79% [2.792 mean])
26. Does purchasing department communicate well with accounts payable and receiving? (0 = —; 1 = —; 2 = 25%; 3 = 75% [2.75 mean])
27. Do accounts payable clerks always have the information that they need from purchasing? (0 = —; 1 = —; 2 = 25%; 3 = 75% [2.75 mean])
28. Do you know what amount of budget is available for all departments in the hospital? (0 = 4%; 1 = 8%; 2 = 34%; 3 = 54% [2.375 mean])

Policies and Procedures:

29. Is there a policy and procedure manual for the department? (0 = —; 1 = —; 2 = 21%; 3 = 79% [2.792 mean])

30. Have you established purchasing standards for the hospital so that all departments are treated equally? (0 = 4%; 1 = 4%; 2 = 46%; 3 = 46% [2.333 mean])
31. Is there a special procedure for purchase of capital equipment? (0 = —; 1 = —; 2 = 46%; 3 = 54% [2.542 mean])
32. Are purchase requisitions required before a purchase order will be filled out? (0 = 4%; 1 = 4%; 2 = 38%; 3 = 54% [2.417 mean])
33. Is there a system available to authorize invoices which do not agree with order on price, terms, or freight? (0 = —; 1 = 8%; 2 = 38%; 3 = 54% [2.458 mean])
34. Is there a hospital standardization committee to control product proliferation? (0 = —; 1 = —; 2 = 58%; 3 = 42% [2.417 mean])
35. Do you utilize any type of economic order quantity procedure? (0 = —; 1 = 4%; 2 = 58%; 3 = 38% [2.333 mean])
36. Do you try to buy products that meet the needs of several departments rather than stocking several brands of nearly identical items? (0 = —; 1 = —; 2 = 21%; 3 = 79% [2.792 mean])
37. Do you try to maintain minimum inventory while minimizing out-of-stock situations? (0 = —; 1 8%; 2 = 17%; 3 = 75% [2.667 mean])
38. Is a value analysis of products ever made to be sure that the product meets the need for which it is intended? (0 = —; 1 = 4%; 2 = 50%; 3 = 46% [2.417 mean])
39. Do you take advantage of quantity discounts when available? (0 = —; 1 = 4%; 2 = 42%; 3 = 54% [2.5 mean])
40. Would it be possible to pool your orders with those of other hospitals in order to obtain quantity discounts? (0 = 4%; 1 = 17%; 2 = 46%; 3 = 33% [2.043 mean])
41. Do you attempt to avoid rush orders? (0 = —; 1 = 12%; 2 = 50%; 3 = 38% [2.25 mean])
42. Do you receive competitive bids from vendors? (0 = —; 1 = 8%; 2 = 42%; 3 = 50% [2.417 mean])
43. Are all provisions of bids considered such as freight terms, discounts, and service? (0 = —; 1 = —; 2 = 33%; 3 = 66% [2.667 mean])
44. Are exceptions to lowest bid allowed? (0 = —; 1 = 4%; 2 = 54%; 3 = 42% [2.375 mean])
    44-A. If yes, how are such exceptions controlled? (0 = —; 1 = 17%; 2 = 48%; 3 = 35% [2.333 mean])
45. Are quotations obtained from several vendors before an order is placed? (0 = —; 1 = 17%; 2 = 48%; 3 = 35% [2.174 mean])
46. Do you feel that quantities purchased are always consistent with actual requirements? (0 = —; 1 = —; 2 = 75%; 3 = 25% [2.25 mean])
47. Do you make purchases from several different sources to insure a steady source of supply? (0 = —; 1 = 38%; 2 = 42%; 3 = 20% [1.833 mean])

48. Is there a follow-up procedure for use on orders not shipped promptly? (0 = —; 1 = 12%; 2 = 42%; 3 = 46% [2.333 mean])
49. Does a special procedure exist when vendors back-order an item? (0 = —; 1 = 21%; 2 = 58%; 3 = 21% [2.0 mean])
50. Do purchase orders normally include prices (0 = —; 1 = 8%; 2 = 21%; 3 = 71% [2.625 mean])
51. Is a record kept of instances when actual purchase price varies from expected purchase price? (0 = 7%; 1 = 21%; 2 = 38%; 3 = 33% [1.958 mean])
52. Do you establish a usage rate on each item in order to maintain proper inventories? (0 = —; 1 = —; 2 = 42%; 3 = 58% [2.583 mean])
53. Do you have a predetermined level of safety stock for items? (0 = —; 1 = 8%; 2 = 29%; 3 = 63% [2.542 mean])
54. Are files periodically purged of old records? (0 = 4%; 1 = 25%; 2 = 50%; 3 = 21% [1.875 mean])

Departmental Staff:

55. Is the departmental staff large enough? (0 = —; 1 = 14%; 2 = 46%; 3 = 50% [2.458 mean])
56. Do you feel that all department employees are highly ethical? (0 = —; 1 = 8%; 2 = 17%; 3 = 75% [2.667 mean])
57. Do employees in the department have a favorable attitude toward their job and the hospital? (0 = —; 1 = 4%; 2 = 33%; 3 = 63% [2.583 mean])
58. Do employees have an adequate knowledge of products handled? (0 = —; 1 = 12%; 2 = 42%; 3 = 46% [2.333 mean])
59. Do employees make an effort to keep informed about new items? (0 = —; 1 = 8%; 2 = 50%; 3 = 42% [2.333 mean])
60. Does the hospital provide for continuing education of employees? (0 = —; 1 = 4%; 2 = 50%; 3 = 46% [2.417 mean])
61. What is the employee turnover rate in the department? (0 = —; 1 = 4%; 2 = 54%; 3 = 42% [2.375 mean])
62. What is the employee absence rate? (0 = —; 1 = 4%; 2 = 54%; 3 = 42% [2.375 mean])

Relations with Vendors:

63. Do you deal only with reputable vendors? (0 = —; 1 = —; 2 = 29%; 3 = 71% [2.708 mean])
64. Do you have vendor performance files that tell you who is dependable in various situations? (0 = 4%; 1 = 29%; 2 = 38%; 3 = 29% [1.917 mean])
65. Is a statement of policies made available to vendors? (0 = —; 1 = 29%; 2 = 38%; 3 = 33% [2.042 mean])
66. Do you make certain that vendors guarantee their products before placing an order? (0 = —; 1 = 12%; 2 = 46%; 3 = 42% [2.292 mean])

67. Are salesmen discouraged from contacting other department heads? (0 = 4%; 1 = 17%; 2 = 29%; 3 = 50% [2.25 mean])
68. Is there any policy with respect to acceptance of gifts from vendors? (0 = 4%; 1 = 12%; 2 = 46%; 3 = 38% [2.167 mean])

Forms and Reports:

69. Are purchase order blanks prenumbered? (0 = 4%; 1 = 8%; 2 = 17%; 3 = 71% [2.542 mean])
70. Is there a combined purchase order and receiving report? (0 = 4%; 1 = 8%; 2 = 38%; 3 = 50% [2.333 mean])
71. Is there sufficient space on all forms (particularly purchase orders) for the information that needs to be recorded on the forms? (0 = —; 1 = 29%; 2 = 38%; 3 = 33% [2.522 mean])
72. Are preprinted forms available for obtaining quotations and bids from vendors? (0 = —; 1 = 29%; 2 = 38%; 3 = 33% [2.042 mean])
73. Is spacing on forms correct for easy typing? (0 = 8%; 1 = 4%; 2 = 42%; 3 = 46% [2.25 mean])
74. Are monthly purchase reports prepared and does anyone read them? (0 = —; 1 = 21%; 2 = 46%; 3 = 33% [2.125 mean])

Appendix F: Operations Audit Questionnaire: Receiving and Materials Handling Department

Note: In a preliminary survey, six departmental managers in 84 hospitals were asked to rate the importance of each question listed below as follows: 0 = Not Important; 1 = Of Minor Importance; 2 = Important; and 3 = Very Important. The percentage of respondents who replied according to these scale rankings are shown in parentheses following each question; the figures in brackets represent the mean importance score for the question. A mean score of 1.0 or more was the criteria for selecting questions for the final questionnaire to be administered to departmental employees in the operations audit model.

General:

1. Is there a centralized receiving function? (0 = —; 1 = —; 2 = 22%; 3 = 78% [2.781 mean])
2. Do all goods that are received come through the receiving department? (0 = —; 1 = 3%; 2 = 26%; 8 = 71% [2.677 mean])
3. Is the department responsive to user demands for products? (0 = 3%; 1 = 13%; 2 = 45%; 3 = 39% [2.194 mean])
4. Is the department kept in neat order at all times? (0 = —; 1 = —; 2 = 59%; 3 = 41% [2.406 mean])
5. Are all materials easily accessible when needed? (0 = —; 1 = 3%; 2 = 53%; 3 = 44% [2.406 mean])
6. Are shelf items arranged in a systematic and efficiently workable manner? (0 = —; 1 = —; 2 = 45%; 3 = 55% [2.548 mean])
7. Can it be said that there is a place for everything and everything is always in its place? (0 = —; 1 = —; 2 = 56%; 3 = 44% [2.438 mean])
8. Are the storerooms conveniently close to the receiving dock? (0 = —; 1 = 3%; 2 = 50%; 3 = 47% [2.438 mean])
9. Has inventory turnover remained constant or increased over the past few years? (0 = 3%; 1 = 6%; 2 = 52%; 3 = 39% [2.258 mean])
10. How often do out-of-stock situations occur? (0 = —; 1 = 9%; 2 = 31%; 3 = 60% [2.5 mean])
11. How often do you receive complaints from departments served? (0 = 3%; 1 = 19%; 2 = 50%; 3 = 28% [2.031 mean])
12. What percentage of inventory is obsolete or no longer used items? (0 = 3%; 1 = 6%; 2 = 50%; 3 = 41% [2.281 mean])
13. Do you try to minimize the period of time between the arrival of a shipment

and delivery to the proper department? (0 = —; 1 = 6%; 2 = 47%; 3 = 47% [2.406 mean])
14. Do you know your cost per receiving report processed? (0 = 3%; 1 = 28%; 2 = 53%; 3 = 16% [1.813 mean])
15. Do you know your cost per material requisition processed? (0 = 3%; 1 = 25%; 2 = 56%; 3 = 16% [1.844 mean])
16. Is the annual physical count of inventory performed by someone other than those responsible for keeping perpetual records? (0 = 13%; 1 = 32%; 2 = 32%; 3 = 23% [1.645 mean])
17. Is a reconciliation prepared between the perpetual inventory records and the yearend inventory physical count? (0 = 30%; 1 = 13%; 2 = 34%; 3 = 50% [2.313 mean])
18. Is there an open line of communication with all departments? (0 = —; 1 = 3%; 2 = 50%; 3 = 47% [2.438 mean])
19. Is there written approval by a responsible employee of adjustment made to perpetual records based upon physical inventory counts? (0 = 6%; 1 = 16%; 2 = 50%; 3 = 28% [2.0 mean])
20. How much was the last adjustment to perpetual inventory resulting from a physical inventory? (0 = 6%; 1 = 9%; 2 = 63%; 3 = 22% [2.0 mean])
21. Are physical inventories taken in cycles (perhaps 1/12 counted each month)? (0 = 13%; 1 = 31%; 2 = 47%; 3 = 9% [1.438 mean])
22. Are all inventories insured? (0 = 6%; 1 = 23%; 2 = 43%; 3 = 28% [1.9 mean])
23. Is there close coordination with the purchasing agent? (0 = —; 1 = —; 2 = 44%; 3 = 56% [2.563 mean])
24. Is there close coordination with the accounting department? (0 = —; 1 = 6%; 2 = 41%; 3 = 53% [2.469 mean])
25. Is a monthly expense report prepared and sent to departments to keep them aware of costs incurred by them? (0 = 6%; 1 = 16%; 2 = 47%; 3 = 31% [2.031 mean])

Procedures:

26. Is there a written set of established receiving procedures? (0 = 3%; 1 = 9%; 2 = 22%; 3 = 66% [2.5 mean])
27. Are formal procedures always followed? (0 = 3%; 1 = 19%; 2 = 66%; 3 = 12% [1.875 mean])
28. Do you feel that all formal procedures are necessary? (0 = 13%; 1 = 28%; 2 = 38%; 3 = 21% [1.688 mean])
29. Are all items counted as they are unloaded? (0 = —; 1 = 3%; 2 = 28%; 3 = 69% [2.656 mean])
30. Are rejected items returned to vendors promptly? (0 = —; 1 = 6%; 2 = 31%; 3 = 63% [2.563 mean])
31. Are shipments checked for damages? (0 = —; 1 = —; 2 = 28%; 3 = 72% [2.719 mean])

32. Are early or over shipments returned to vendors? (0 = 9%; 1 = 22%; 2 = 38%; 3 = 31% [1.906 mean])
33. Do you inspect goods for specifications and quality? (0 = 9%; 1 = 22%; 2 = 28%; 3 = 41% [2.0 mean])
34. Is a perpetual inventory system used? (0 = 6%; 1 = 16%; 2 = 34%; 3 = 44% [2.156 mean])
35. Is a requisition required before any materials are given out? (0 = —; 1 = 3%; 2 = 31%; 3 = 66% [2.65 mean])
36. Do you have a hospital catalog with catalog numbers for every item in the warehouse? (0 = 9%; 1 = 25%; 2 = 38%; 3 = 28% [1.844 mean])
37. Are only department heads (or other qualified persons) permitted to requisition materials? (0 = —; 1 = 16%; 2 = 44%; 3 = 40% [2.25 mean])
38. Are files ever purged of old unneeded documents? (0 = —; 1 = 28%; 2 = 53%; 3 = 19% [1.906 mean])
39. Is there a system for reacquiring reusable supplies from user areas within the hospital? (0 = 9%; 1 = 19%; 2 = 53%; 3 = 19% [1.813 mean])
40. Has an efficient procedure been established for routine ordering of supplies by various departments so that the workload in filling orders is distributed evenly throughout the week? (0 = —; 1 = 3%; 2 = 50%; 3 = 47% [2.438 mean])
41. Has a system for automatic floor stocking been established? (0 = 6%; 1 = 22%; 2 = 38%; 3 = 34% [2.0 mean])
42. Is there an efficient method in use for rotation of stock so that the oldest items always go out first? (0 = —; 1 = 3%; 2 = 41%; 3 = 56% [2.531 mean])
43. Are packages date-stamped upon receipt in order to determine time lapse between receipt and delivery to the user? (0 = 13%; 1 = 38%; 2 = 34%; 3 = 15% [1.531 mean])
44. Is there any type of follow-up procedure on back-ordered items? (0 = —; 1 = —; 2 = 53%; 3 = 47% [2.469 mean])
45. Are items which are radioactive, perishable, or require controlled temperatures always delivered immediately to the user? (0 = —; 1 = —; 2 = 28%; 3 = 78% [2.719 mean])
46. Does your filing system provide for easy retrieval of forms upon receipt of merchandise? (0 = —; 1 = 9%; 2 = 38%; 3 = 53% [2.438 mean])
47. Do you try to keep the more frequently called for items at the most easily accessible points in the department? (0 = —; 1 = 6%; 2 = 69%; 3 = 25% [2.188 mean])
48. Have economic order quantities been determined? (0 = 3%; 1 = 6%; 2 = 50%; 3 = 41% [2.281 mean])
49. Are costs ever analyzed to determine whether cost of warehousing can be offset by quantity discounts on large volume purchases? (0 = —; 1 = 9%; 2 = 53%; 3 = 38% [2.281 mean])
50. Is a code system used on purchase orders that will enable receiving personnel to know whether received goods are to be delivered direct to a user

department or placed in inventory? (0 = 3%; 1 = 19%; 2 = 44%; 3 = 34% [2.094 mean])
51. Are reorder points and economic order quantities ever recalculated? (0 = —; 1 = 13%; 2 = 59%; 3 = 28% [2.156 mean])
52. Are lists of slow moving materials ever prepared? (0 = 9%; 1 = 25%; 2 = 44%; 3 = 22% [1.781 mean])
53. Are obsolete or no longer used items disposed of periodically? (0 = 6%; 1 = 16%; 2 = 44%; 3 = 34% [2.063 mean])

Departmental Personnel:

54. Is the department adequately staffed? (0 = —; 1 = 6%; 2 = 41%; 3 = 53% [2.469 mean])
55. Are new employees properly trained? (0 = —; 1 = —; 2 = 38%; 3 = 62% [2.625 mean])
56. Are there written job descriptions for each position in the department? (0 = —; 1 = 6%; 2 = 50%; 3 = 44% [2.375 mean])
57. Do departmental employees have a good attitude about their job and the hospital? (0 = —; 1 = —; 2 = 47%; 3 = 53% [2.531 mean])
58. Do all employees in the department have an adequate knowledge of the materials being handled? (0 = —; 1 = 9%; 2 = 53%; 3 = 38% [2.281 mean])
59. Is there a level of intelligence and training present that can improvise when no precedent or policy is available? (0 = —; 1 = 13%; 2 = 56%; 3 = 31% [2.188 mean])
60. Is access to storeroom restricted to specific employees? (0 = —; 1 = 3%; 2 = 35%; 3 = 62% [2.581 mean])
61. Are departmental employees bonded in case of theft? (0 = 10%; 1 = 29%; 2 = 35%; 3 = 26% [1.774 mean])
62. What is the employee turnover rate? (0 = 3%; 1 = 16%; 2 = 58%; 3 = 23% [2.0 mean])
63. What is the employee absence rate? (0 = 3%; 1 = 10%; 2 = 64%; 3 = 23% [2.065 mean])

Physical Facilities:

64. Are the physical facilities adequate? (0 = 3%; 1 = 3%; 2 = 41%; 3 = 53% [2.438 mean])
65. Is there sufficient equipment within the department? (0 = —; 1 = 3%; 2 = 50%; 3 = 47% [2.438 mean])
66. Is storage space adequate? (0 = —; 1 = 3%; 2 = 34%; 3 = 63% [2.594 mean])
67. Are aisles wide enough? (0 = —; 1 = 6%; 2 = 50%; 3 = 44% [2.375 mean])
68. Is there an item location file that permits easy finding of any item quickly? (0 = —; 1 = 16%; 2 = 66%; 3 = 18% [2.031 mean])

69. Is there an adequate supply of fire extinguishers? (0 = —; 1 = 3%; 2 = 25%; 3 = 72% [2.688 mean])
70. Is a burglar alarm system used? (0 = 9%; 1 = 34%; 2 = 34%; 3 = 23% [1.688 mean])

Forms and Reports:

71. Are receiving reports sent to Purchasing and Accounting immediately after the goods are received? (0 = —; 1 = 6%; 2 = 44%; 3 = 50% [2.438 mean])
72. Do receiving reports and material requisition forms have adequate space for all information that should be recorded? (0 = —; 1 = 6%; 2 = 69%; 3 = 25% [2.188 mean])
73. Are all forms the proper size for easy filing? (0 = 3%; 1 = 19%; 2 = 56%; 3 = 22% [1.969 mean])

Appendix G: Operations Audit Test Cases: Survey Memoranda and Audit Reports

Note: The Survey Memoranda and Audit Reports for two hospital operations audits, which were conducted to test the model and accompanying questionnaires described in Chapter 4 and 5, appear on the following pages. The hospital names, the actual audit workpapers, and the questionnaires are not shown because of the confidential nature of some of the material.

Survey Memorandum: Hospital A

Physical Tour

After a short discussion with the controller, a physical tour was conducted of the six departments being audited. Accounting appeared to have a multitude of problems as seven different questions on the physical tour questionnaire were answered negatively for that department. The number of negative responses for the other departments were as follows:

Patient Census Management, 4;
Personnel, 3;
Payroll, 2;
Receiving and Materials Handling, 1;
Purchasing, 0.

Acquisition of Written Data

The acquisition of data stage presented a minor impediment since some of the data (see list in Chapter 4) were not available. For example, there were no written goals and objectives, policies and procedures manuals, job descriptions, budgets, internal departmental reports, monthly financial statements (yearend statements were prepared by a CPA firm), HAS Reports, or flow charts.

The first three items listed above indicate deficiencies in all departments. The remainder relate to the accounting department. Consequently, this stage of the audit indicated that problems existed in the accounting department.

Preliminary Management Questions

The management questions resulted in some negative responses for all departments with accounting receiving the most. The total number of negative responses for each department were as follows:

Accounting, 21;
Personnel, 15;
Purchasing, 15;
Receiving and Materials Handling, 10;
Patient Census Management, 8;
Payroll, 7.

Conclusions

The results of all stages of the audit indicated that the accounting department would be a logical choice for the in-depth stage of the audit.

Note: The departmental questionnaire for accounting was utilized and the results were the basis for the audit report. Purely for test purposes, the questionnaires for the remaining five departments were also used in the appropriate departments. No audit report was prepared for these latter five departments. The results in these five departments corresponded with the preliminary stage of the audit in that no major problems were unearthed. The results of the in-depth audit of the accounting department culminated in an audit report. The exit review with the controller resulted in his total agreement with the audit report.

Audit Report: Hospital A

1. There is no procedures manual (Accounting Manual) for the department. The availability of a procedures manual, complete with job descriptions and a written internal control system could result in improved department operations.

2. Monthly financial statements were not prepared. The availability of monthly statements coupled with a budget system might encourage all department heads to perform as expected.

3. Bank statements were not reconciled monthly. By eliminating the bank reconciliation from the duties of the audit firm, the controller would be more aware of the financial pulse of the organization.

4. Another important factor to determine is the policy of taking all cash discounts for early payment as well as the reasons for discounts lost.

5. Control accounts were not regularly reconciled with the subsidiary ledgers. Regular reconciliation would uncover errors as they are committed rather than permitting a problem situation to develop. This condition was true in receivables, payables, and fixed assets.

6. There should be some control placed upon the use of the copying machine. A monthly tabulation of its use would assist in determining whether a problem exists or not.

7. Some of the questionnaire responses indicated that there was some problem with employee morale.

Survey Memorandum: Hospital B

Physical Tour

The physical tour resulted in little in the way of irregularities. Two questions on the auditor's list of questions received negative responses for patient census management. Personnel and purchasing received one negative response each. There were no negative responses for the remaining three departments.

Acquisition of Written Data

All necessary written data was examined with the exception of financial information. At this hospital, financial statements and budgets were not made available to anyone under any circumstances. Information was provided that the financial statements did show that revenues exceeded expenses. The written data that was examined appeared to be quite adequate and no irregularities were noted.

Preliminary Management Questions

The managerial personnel reacted affirmatively to most questions. The total number of negative responses for each department were as follows:

Patient Census Management, 8;
Personnel, 5;
Payroll, 5;
Purchasing, 4;
Receiving and Materials Handling, 3;
Accounting, 2.

Conclusions

Although all six departments appeared to be operating with few problems, the patient census management department was selected for the in-depth audit. This selection was based primarily on the number of negative responses received for the physical tour questions and the preliminary management questions.

Note: The in-depth audit was conducted and resulted in the following audit report. It should be noted that the problem areas noted in the audit report were all quite minor. After discussion with the department head, it was discovered that he was already familiar with all of the problems and work was in process to institute changes.

Audit Report: Hospital B

1. There should be some control placed upon the use of the copying machine. A monthly tabulation of its use would assist in determining whether a problem exists.
2. No record is kept of the reasons for long distance telephone calls. If a permanent record were required, the number of unnecessary and personal telephone calls might be reduced.
3. Most departmental employees seem to think that there is a shortage of waiting room space near the department. Since an increase in space may not be possible in the near future, it might be appropriate to handle pre-admissions by mail or over the telephone.
4. Although the bad debt expense is less than the national average, there is still room for improvement. Answers to the questionnaires indicated that nothing is done to discourage pseudo-emergencies, charge cards are not accepted, and deposits from patients are not always obtained prior to admission. A change in any of these policies could lead to a reduction in bad debt costs.

Appendix H: Sample Hospital Advisory Services (HAS) Report

SIX MONTH MEDIANS FOR THE PERIOD ENDING DECEMBER 31, 1972

HOSPITALS 100 THRU 149

	REGION 1	REGION 2	REGION 3	REGION 4	REGION 5	REGION 6	REGION 7	REGION 8	REGION 9
INPATIENT-REVENUE PER PATIENT DAY	95.66	85.56	76.41	84.60	78.46	74.42	79.17	103.80	124.17
-COST PER PATIENT DAY RCCAC	90.78	82.52	71.16	81.48	70.35	74.17	73.24	96.02	123.77
-COST PER STAY RCCAC	653.03	609.30	479.28	581.87	442.54	526.49	474.68	521.32	671.75
DAYS OF REVENUE IN PATIENT ACCTS. REC.	87.66	70.00	77.32	70.04	81.92	67.93	77.17	82.80	76.46
RESERVE A PERCENT OF ACCTS. REC.	13.99	13.05	21.41	15.00	16.12	14.05	16.97	13.38	15.96
ALL NURSING UNITS-EXPENSE PERCENT	26.23	25.18	25.34	26.58	27.18	27.61	26.66	23.49	25.27
-PERCENT OF OCCUPANCY	77.52	76.69	78.96	71.17	74.20	67.52	71.84	66.29	64.70
-LENGTH OF STAY	7.07	7.72	6.64	7.08	6.32	7.07	6.34	5.48	5.52
-DIRECT EXPENSE PER PATIENT DAY	27.70	23.39	20.41	24.02	19.71	22.52	20.57	25.30	32.90
-MANHOURS PER PATIENT DAY	7.02	5.64	6.35	6.52	6.71	6.51	6.74	6.75	6.92
HOL.VAC.SICK PAY PERCENT OF SALARIES	8.94	8.33	7.45	8.06	6.91	7.23	6.82	7.08	9.15
FULL TIME EMPLOYEE PER-OCCUPIED BED	3.14	2.67	2.78	2.80	2.81	2.68	2.84	3.35	3.45
-BED	2.48	1.90	2.10	1.97	2.08	1.72	2.06	2.18	1.99
HOSPITAL UTILIZATION INDEX	3.46	3.16	3.57	3.16	3.69	2.87	3.43	3.62	3.78
-------- REVENUE PERCENTAGES --------									
OBSTETRICAL SUITE	6.3	5.3	4.8	5.3	3.2	5.0	3.3	5.4	5.0
MEDICAL + SURGICAL NURSING UNITS	48.2	45.7	42.8	44.6	40.7	43.9	40.3	38.1	37.9
INTENSIVE AND CORONARY CARE UNITS	3.8	2.7	2.5	3.1	1.9	2.9	2.9	3.1	5.0
OPERATING AND RECOVERY ROOMS	6.0	5.6	5.6	4.8	4.7	5.3	4.5	6.7	8.8
CENTRAL SERVICES + SUPPLY	1.5	1.9	3.7	3.5	3.8	4.1	4.0	4.6	3.8
INTRAVENOUS THERAPY	1.4	1.4	2.1	2.2	1.6	1.9	1.9	1.8	1.5
EMERGENCY SERVICES	4.6	2.3	3.4	2.2	1.4	1.2	1.5	1.9	3.2
LABORATORY-INPATIENT	7.2	9.6	9.8	9.2	10.4	10.0	10.4	9.8	8.9
-OUTPATIENT	2.5	0.8	1.4	1.1	1.4	1.2	1.7	1.7	0.9
BLOOD BANK	0.3	0.4	0.5	0.4	0.5	0.4	0.6	0.4	0.5
RADIOLOGY-INPATIENT	2.8	5.0	4.8	4.7	5.4	5.3	6.2	4.7	3.9
-OUTPATIENT	4.2	4.2	2.7	3.1	1.8	0.8	1.8	3.1	3.1
PHARMACY	3.8	5.2	8.6	6.5	9.6	7.9	11.1	6.8	6.9
ANESTHESIOLOGY	1.1	2.5	2.7	2.7	2.4	2.3	2.5	1.7	1.2
INHALATION THERAPY	2.1	1.9	2.0	2.7	2.6	2.0	3.2	3.3	3.2
PHYSICAL THERAPY	0.9	0.8	0.7	1.5	1.1	1.4	1.3	1.4	1.1
CLINICS	0.0	2.0	2.0	1.5	1.3	1.6	0.0	0.0	0.0
ALL OTHER PATIENT SERVICES	2.0	2.0	2.0	1.5	1.3	1.6	1.9	1.5	2.0
GROSS INPATIENT REVENUE	86.6	88.2	90.6	91.1	94.2	93.6	94.2	91.4	88.7
GROSS OUTPATIENT REVENUE	12.9	11.2	9.3	8.8	5.7	6.2	5.7	8.5	9.9
TOTAL PATIENT REVENUE	0.0	0.0	0.0	0.0	0.0	0.0	0.0	0.0	0.0
DEDUCTIONS FROM PATIENT REVENUE	-7.7	-12.5	-9.2	-5.4	-11.6	-4.4	-6.7	-7.6	-6.0
ALL OTHER REPORTED REVENUE	5.1	2.5	2.8	2.4	2.8	2.9	2.7	2.6	2.0

113

SIX MONTH MEDIANS FOR THE PERIOD ENDING DECEMBER 31, 1972

HOSPITALS 100 THRU 149

	REGION 1	REGION 2	REGION 3	REGION 4	REGION 5	REGION 6	REGION 7	REGION 8	REGION 9
NURSING ADM.-EXPENSE PERCENT	2.1	2.1	1.7	2.0	1.1	2.1	1.5	2.3	2.2
-MANHOURS PER BED	10.21	8.56	6.40	7.18	4.80	7.57	7.00	10.69	9.93
------OBSTETRICAL SUITE------									
OBSTETRICAL UNIT-EXPENSE PERCENT	2.1	1.8	1.9	2.3	1.7	2.4	1.7	2.3	1.9
-PERCENT OCCUPANCY	50.83	51.83	54.70	44.79	49.66	44.10	42.00	43.00	48.66
-PERCENT OF TOTAL ADMISSIONS	12.24	14.11	16.00	11.76	10.82	11.29	10.04	12.16	14.32
-AVERAGE LENGTH OF STAY	4.14	3.92	3.32	3.66	3.92	3.76	3.29	3.11	2.97
-OBSTETRICAL TURNOVER RATE	3.72	3.83	4.41	3.71	4.00	3.41	4.00	4.25	4.78
-NURSING MH PER PATIENT DAY	9.65	5.63	5.76	8.35	7.91	8.21	7.24	7.96	7.62
DEL.+ LABOR ROOMS-EXPENSE PERCENT	1.1	0.8	1.1	0.6	1.3	0.4	0.7	0.5	1.1
-DELIVERY+LABOR MH PER DELIVERY	14.23	10.94	9.69	8.92	16.54	8.00	6.85	6.60	14.61
NURSERY UNIT-EXPENSE PERCENT	1.0	1.0	1.1	0.8	0.8	1.1	0.9	1.3	1.1
-NURSING MH PER NEWBORN DAY	4.56	4.04	4.71	4.39	4.39	4.96	5.86	5.44	4.57
OBSTETRICAL SUITE DIR. EXP. PER STAY	258.20	175.50	148.96	196.86	180.67	175.47	151.08	212.05	204.25
------MEDICAL SURGICAL NURSING UNITS------									
MED.+SURG.UNITS-EXPENSE PERCENT	22.4	21.0	22.3	21.3	23.7	22.2	22.5	19.6	20.0
-PERCENT OCCUPANCY	81.28	80.60	80.71	75.39	75.10	71.19	76.55	68.95	65.90
-AVERAGE LENGTH OF STAY	7.37	8.18	7.18	7.50	6.33	7.55	6.72	5.94	5.78
-MED.+SURG. TURNOVER RATE	3.00	2.68	3.28	2.81	3.56	2.65	3.36	3.37	3.32
-NURSING MH PER PATIENT DAY	6.82	5.22	5.90	6.11	6.54	6.20	6.41	6.48	6.28
RN MANHOURS PER PATIENT DAY	2.46	2.35	1.46	1.60	1.38	1.71	0.78	1.84	2.35
LPN MANHOURS PER PATIENT DAY	1.39	1.31	1.36	0.89	1.85	1.11	1.95	1.60	1.63
OTHER MH PER PATIENT DAY	2.33	1.63	3.01	3.22	2.97	3.60	3.07	2.58	2.23
-PERCENT REGISTERED NURSES	37.76	39.39	23.31	29.96	20.22	26.05	13.68	34.85	37.93
-PERCENT LICENSED PRACTICAL NURSES	22.70	27.68	23.49	15.52	26.24	18.00	33.04	27.18	21.99
-AVERAGE HOURLY SALARY	3.22	3.07	2.65	2.97	2.52	2.68	2.48	2.91	3.63
REGISTERED NURSES	4.06	3.88	3.79	4.25	3.97	4.05	4.06	3.89	4.64
LICENSED PRACTICAL NURSES	3.17	2.91	2.63	3.11	2.64	2.84	2.51	2.69	3.06
OTHER NURSING PERSONNEL	2.31	2.46	2.06	2.27	2.10	2.10	1.86	2.29	2.60
-INTENSIVE AND CORONARY CARE UNITS									
PERCENT OCCUPANCY	63.03	71.33	52.12	56.00	44.66	45.83	44.44	54.33	58.88
MANHOURS PER PATIENT DAY	16.52	13.16	16.45	19.40	19.23	17.45	21.64	18.33	15.63
SALARY PER PATIENT DAY	68.67	53.76	57.87	71.22	66.76	67.16	61.48	70.65	67.05
AVERAGE HOURLY SALARY	3.87	4.05	3.64	3.80	3.47	3.59	3.02	3.79	4.36
PERCENT OF TOTAL M+S BEDS	6.00	4.37	5.26	4.30	4.28	4.02	4.44	4.58	7.00
SALARY EXPENSE PER PATIENT DAY	23.42	19.76	17.03	19.85	17.31	17.94	17.33	20.51	25.82

SIX MONTH MEDIANS FOR THE PERIOD ENDING DECEMBER 31,1972

HOSPITALS 100 THRU 149

	REGION 1	REGION 2	REGION 3	REGION 4	REGION 5	REGION 6	REGION 7	REGION 8	REGION 9
OPERATING ROOMS-EXPENSE PERCENT	3.2	3.7	3.6	3.2	3.6	3.5	3.6	4.2	4.8
-O.R. VISITS/100 M+S ADMISSIONS	46.57	56.48	45.62	42.15	32.30	44.22	32.97	52.04	58.14
-MANHOURS PER O.R. VISIT	10.82	8.86	9.81	10.30	12.97	9.69	10.93	9.59	9.75
RECOVERY ROOMS-EXPENSE PERCENT	0.3	0.3	0.4	0.4	0.5	0.4	0.4	0.4	0.3
CENTRAL SERVICES-EXPENSE PERCENT	1.9	2.1	2.4	2.2	2.3	2.6	2.6	2.4	1.9
-LINE ITEMS PER MANHOUR	4.70	4.60	4.31	4.76	5.06	4.37	4.08	4.52	3.46
-LINE ITEMS PER PATIENT DAY	0.87	1.27	1.10	1.47	1.58	1.27	1.10	1.55	1.64
INTRAVENOUS THERAPY-EXPENSE PERCENT	0.7	0.6	0.7	0.5	0.4	0.6	0.6	0.7	0.8
EMERGENCY SERVICE-EXPENSE PERCENT	2.6	1.7	2.1	1.5	1.0	0.7	1.1	1.2	2.2
-MANHOURS PER VISIT	1.13	1.11	1.25	1.23	0.98	0.94	1.20	1.29	1.45
NURSING EDUCATION-EXPENSE PERCENT	0.5	1.1	0.4	0.4	0.3	0.6	0.6	0.4	0.5
CLINIC-EXPENSE PERCENT	0.5	0.1	0.0	0.5	0.0	0.0	0.0	0.4	0.0
-MANHOURS PER VISIT	0.93	0.59	0.00	0.39	0.00	0.00	0.00	0.00	0.00
LABORATORY EXPENSE PERCENT	7.2	7.6	7.2	8.0	7.2	7.1	6.6	7.8	7.1
-TESTS PER ADMISSION	19.15	19.79	15.06	17.33	13.65	17.75	18.36	15.76	18.13
-TESTS PER MANHOUR	4.62	4.38	4.18	4.32	4.28	5.00	4.13	3.66	4.43
-WEIGHTED UNITS PER MANHOUR	35.76	22.28	39.76	27.67	15.71	40.55	30.17	36.71	35.16
-DIRECT EXPENSE EX FEES- PER TEST	1.52	1.44	1.67	1.66	2.02	1.37	1.86	1.86	1.71
-PER WEIGHTED UNIT	0.21	0.41	0.22	0.27	0.50	0.13	0.15	0.19	0.21
-PERCENT OP TESTS	25.62	16.10	14.11	13.96	4.07	6.95	7.12	11.81	11.48
BLOOD BANK-EXPENSE PERCENT	0.4	0.4	0.5	0.5	0.4	0.4	0.5	0.3	0.3
-MANHOURS PER UNIT DRAWN	0.00	3.13	1.79	2.48	0.00	0.00	1.00	0.00	0.00
RADIOLOGY-EXPENSE PERCENT	5.5	6.2	5.5	5.5	4.0	5.6	5.5	6.0	5.3
-DIAGNOSTIC PROCEDURES PER ADM.	1.52	1.55	1.60	1.79	1.57	1.52	1.64	1.47	1.21
-DIRECT EXPENSE PER PROCED EX-FEE	7.10	7.34	6.07	6.55	6.59	6.66	7.38	7.88	9.76
-MANHOURS PER PROCEDURE	0.98	1.13	1.12	1.01	1.27	1.03	1.16	1.05	1.22
-PERCENT OP PROCEDURES	59.50	52.30	44.72	43.84	23.73	35.70	25.62	36.13	44.92
PHARMACY-EXPENSE PERCENT	2.7	2.9	4.0	3.6	4.8	4.0	5.1	3.7	3.1
-LINE ITEMS PER MANHOUR	6.98	9.93	10.68	9.61	7.10	11.22	11.42	12.77	9.15
-LINE ITEMS PER PATIENT DAY	1.29	1.11	1.85	1.73	1.52	1.59	2.26	3.26	2.38
ANESTHESIOLOGY-EXPENSE PERCENT	0.5	1.6	1.9	1.4	1.7	1.7	1.8	0.4	0.6
INHALATION THERAPY-EXPENSE PERCENT	1.1	0.7	1.0	1.3	1.4	0.9	1.2	1.5	1.6
PHYSICAL THERAPY-EXPENSE PERCENT	0.4	0.6	0.5	0.9	0.7	0.7	0.8	0.8	0.8
-DIRECT EXPENSE PER TREATMENT	3.87	3.55	3.30	3.26	2.99	3.01	3.56	3.97	4.27
-TREATMENTS PER MANHOUR	1.13	1.33	1.35	1.66	1.73	1.31	1.44	1.29	1.21
SOCIAL SERVICE-EXPENSE PERCENT	0.3	0.3	0.2	0.2	0.0	0.1	0.1	0.2	0.2
-MANHOURS PER CASE ACCEPTED	5.83	7.79	5.64	3.70	0.00	0.00	0.00	7.21	2.48
MEDICAL RECORDS-EXPENSE PERCENT	1.3	1.3	1.3	1.3	1.3	1.2	1.3	1.3	1.3
-MANHOURS PER DISCHARGE UNIT	2.60	2.31	2.17	2.50	2.00	2.31	2.20	2.61	2.69
-DIRECT EXPENSE PER DISCHARGE UNIT	8.87	8.27	7.05	7.97	6.26	7.13	6.73	8.01	10.09
MEDICAL LIBRARY-EXPENSE PERCENT	0.0	0.0	0.0	0.1	0.0	0.0	0.0	0.0	0.2
OTHER PAT. SERVICES-EXPENSE PERCENT	1.1	0.8	0.8	0.8	0.6	0.7	0.7	0.8	0.8

SIX MONTH MEDIANS FOR THE PERIOD ENDING DECEMBER 31,1972

HOSPITALS 100 THRU 149

	REGION 1	REGION 2	REGION 3	REGION 4	REGION 5	REGION 6	REGION 7	REGION 8	REGION 9
DIETARY-EXPENSE PERCENT	7.7	8.5	7.7	7.7	8.0	7.6	7.7	6.8	5.9
TOTAL-MEALS PER PATIENT DAY	4.10	4.03	4.11	4.19	4.54	4.38	4.14	4.12	4.09
-DIRECT EXPENSE PER MEAL	2.00	1.56	1.44	1.65	1.45	1.48	1.43	1.67	1.84
-SALARY EXPENSE PER MEAL	0.90	0.81	0.74	0.89	0.70	0.82	0.69	0.87	0.99
-MEALS SERVED PER MANHOUR	2.55	2.84	2.92	2.74	3.00	2.68	2.83	2.45	2.96
INPATIENT MEALS SERVED PPD	2.79	2.86	2.89	2.83	2.78	2.74	2.84	2.71	2.67
CAFETERIA MEALS-PERCENT OF TOTAL	33.03	28.48	29.27	34.16	39.82	35.75	31.96	33.08	35.61
-PER MANHOUR	3.93	4.66	5.58	5.59	5.96	6.25	5.28	4.52	6.67
PLANT ENGINEERING-EXPENSE PERCENT	4.6	5.1	4.7	5.2	5.4	5.4	4.4	4.4	4.0
-DIRECT EXPENSE PER 1000 FEET	136.76	155.18	139.68	152.04	151.77	131.18	125.79	136.43	144.81
-MANHOURS PER 1000 FEET	19.27	16.74	17.71	16.57	15.48	13.77	14.51	16.91	15.36
-SQUARE FEET PER BED	732.09	692.52	584.09	702.72	637.41	586.62	629.31	712.66	736.92
HOUSEKEEPING-EXPENSE PERCENT	3.7	3.6	3.5	3.5	3.7	3.7	3.8	2.6	3.1
-DIRECT EXPENSE PER 1000 FEET	141.53	110.48	128.11	114.88	117.88	103.05	121.59	85.11	140.64
-MANHOURS PER 1000FEET	49.50	41.99	53.13	41.15	51.28	38.93	49.10	34.57	43.60
-SQUARE FEET PER BED	624.42	512.66	465.95	536.14	525.58	531.58	532.00	641.40	586.90
LAUNDRY + LINEN-EXPENSE PERCENT	1.9	1.7	1.8	1.9	1.6	1.8	1.8	1.9	1.9
-LAUNDRY EXPENSE PER 100 POUNDS	10.71	9.96	9.45	10.13	8.07	8.19	9.67	9.69	10.74
-LAUNDRY POUNDS PER MANHOUR	23.41	32.09	30.78	28.01	28.08	32.42	26.00	30.60	44.34
-POUNDS PER PATIENT DAY	15.22	13.01	11.44	13.78	12.80	14.31	12.13	15.75	17.66
-LINEN EXPENSE PER PATIENT DAY	0.48	0.29	0.32	0.32	0.25	0.18	0.26	0.50	0.58
ADM. + FISCAL-EXPENSE PERCENT	10.8	11.1	10.7	10.7	10.8	10.1	10.3	12.0	11.9
-ADMINISTRATION MANHOURS PER BED	29.10	15.09	26.29	18.38	14.13	16.95	16.12	12.35	14.45
-FISCAL SERVICES MANHOURS PER BED	24.46	26.67	36.90	27.01	27.96	22.85	26.16	35.65	36.07
EMP. HEALTH + WELFARE-EXPENSE PERCENT	4.7	5.0	5.0	5.8	4.3	4.5	4.2	4.5	5.6
-PERCENT OF SALARIES	7.21	8.76	8.97	9.98	8.20	7.93	7.71	8.58	9.89
DEPRECIATION-EXPENSE PERCENT	3.6	4.6	3.5	4.3	4.4	4.9	3.8	4.7	4.4
MISC. OPERATING-EXPENSE PERCENT	0.8	0.9	0.8	1.3	0.4	1.7	0.4	3.5	1.8
--HOSPITAL 100 PERCENT BASE TOTAL	0.0	0.0	0.0	0.0	0.0	0.0	0.0	0.0	0.0
-SALARIES A PERCENT OF TOTAL EXP.	59.5	56.6	56.4	56.9	55.4	57.6	55.6	54.8	54.2
-PROF. FEES PERCENT OF TOTAL EXP.	3.2	5.4	4.4	5.1	4.4	4.4	3.4	4.0	3.5
-OTHER DIRECT EXPENSE PERCENT	35.7	38.3	37.7	38.4	40.0	38.6	40.1	41.3	41.0
-----ADDITIONAL PROGRAMS-------									
MEDICAL STAFF-EXPENSE PERCENT	3.7	2.0	2.1	1.0	4.3	1.0	0.7	1.0	2.6
RESEARCH EXPENSE PERCENT	0.0	0.0	0.0	0.0	0.0	0.0	0.0	0.0	0.0
PERSONNEL QUARTERS-EXPENSE PERCENT	0.0	0.2	0.2	0.0	0.0	0.0	0.0	0.0	0.0
MISC. NON-OPERATING EXPENSE	1.5	0.4	0.8	0.7	0.0	0.6	0.7	1.3	0.8

Notes

Notes

Notes to Chapter 1
Introduction

1. Joann S. Lublin, "Outfit That Accredits Hospitals Helps Set Quality of Patient Care," *Wall Street Journal* January 13, 1975, p. 1.
2. Aaron Schneider, "What Operational Auditing Is—And Isn't." *The Internal Auditor* XXX (September-October 1973), p. 10.
3. Roy A. Lindberg and Theodore Cohn, *Operations Auditing* (New York: American Management Association, 1972), p. 16.
4. Anton Steven, "Operational Audits of Construction Contracts," *The Internal Auditor* XXX (May-June 1973), p. 10.
5. Lindberg and Cohn, *Operations Auditing*, p. 16.
6. Robert Edward George Nicol, "An Inquiry into the Problems of Definition and Measurement in Operations Auditing by Professional Accountants," unpublished Ph.D. dissertation, Department of Business Administration, University of California, 1969, p. 6.
7. Ronald S. Brown, CPA, "The Operational Audit," *The Lester Witte Report* V (No. 4, 1974), p. 1.
8. Neil Doppelt, "Operational Auditing and the Management Letter," *Journal of Accountancy* CXXXII (August 1971), p. 82.
9. Nicol, "An Inquiry into the Problems."
10. Edwin Clarence Bomeli, "The Audit of Management Performance," unpublished Ph.D. dissertation, Department of Accounting, Michigan State University, 1963.
11. R.K. Mautz and Hussein A. Sharaf, *The Philosophy of Auditing* (Evanston, Ill.: American Accounting Association, 1961).

Notes to Chapter 2
Operations Auditing

1. George Melloan, "Inside Auditors Widen Role as 'Eyes and Ears' for Top Management," *Wall Street Journal* October 26, 1964, p. 1.
2. R. Gene Brown, "Changing Audit Objectives and Techniques," *Accounting Review* XXXVII (October 1962), p. 696.
3. James Michael Lahey, "Evolution of the Concept of an Audit in Authoritative Professional Literature," unpublished Ph.D. dissertation, Department of Accounting, University of Illinois, 1969, p. 15.
4. Ibid., p. 19.
5. R.H. Montgomery, *Auditing Theory and Practice* (New York: The Ronald Press, 1912), p. 9.

6. Frederick B. Andrews, "Compulsory Audit of Corporations," *Journal of Accountancy* LIV (November 1932), p. 354.

7. *Auditing Standards and Procedures*, Statements on Auditing Standards No. 33 (New York: American Institute of Certified Public Accountants, Inc., 1963).

8. Larry Gene Pointer, "Internal Auditing Comes of Age," *The Internal Auditor* XXX (September-October 1973), p. 35.

9. Ronald S. Brown, CPA, "The Operational Audit," *Lester Witte Report* V (No. 4, 1974), p. 1.

10. Howard F. Stettler, *Systems Based Independent Audits*, 2nd ed. (Englewood Cliffs, N.J.: Prentice-Hall, 1974), p. 78.

11. *Internal Auditing*, Studies in Business Policy, No. 111 (New York: National Industrial Conference Board, Inc., 1963), p. 9.

12. Ibid., p. 4.

13. Ibid.

14. *Statement of Responsibilities of the Internal Auditor* (5500 Diplomat Circle, Orlando, Fla.: Institute of Internal Auditors, 1957).

15. Lawrence B. Sawyer, *Modern Internal Auditing* (Orlando, Fla.: Institute of Internal Auditors, 1973).

16. Lawrence B. Sawyer, "Just What is Management Auditing?" *The Internal Auditor* XXX (March-April 1973), pp. 10-21.

17. *Internal Auditing*, No. 111, p. 5.

18. Ibid.

19. *Standards for Audit of Governmental Organizations, Programs, Activities & Functions* (Washington, D.C.: U.S. Government Printing Office, 1974), p. i.

20. Ibid., p. 1.

21. Ibid., p. 2.

22. *Illinois' Use of Public Accountants for Auditing State Activities* (Washington, D.C.: U.S. Government Printing Office, 1973), p. i.

23. *Examples of Findings From Government Audits* (Washington, D.C.: U.S. Government Printing Office, 1973).

24. Arthur W. Holmes and Wayne S. Overmyer, *Auditing Principles and Procedures* (Homewood, Ill.: Richard D. Irwin, 1971), p. 133.

25. J. Brooks Heckert and James D. Wilson, *Controllership* (New York: Ronald Press, 1963), p. 671.

26. Bradford Camus, *Operational Auditing Handbook* (New York: Institute of Internal Auditors, 1964), p. 51.

27. Neil C. Churchill and Richard M. Cyert, "An Experiment in Management Auditing," *Journal of Accountancy* CXXI (February 1966), p. 39.

28. Harold Q. Langenderfer and Jack C. Robertson, "A Theoretical Structure for Independent Audits of Management," *Accounting Review* XLIV (October 1969), p. 777.

29. Brown, "The Operational Audit," p. 1.

30. Lindberg and Cohn, *Operations Auditing*, p. 9.

31. E.R. Evans, "Some Benefits of Operational Auditing," *The Internal Auditor* XXVI (March-April 1969), p. 47.

32. J. Santocki, "Management Audit—Chance, Challenge, or Lost Opportunity," *The Accountant* CLXX (January 3, 1974), p. 16.

33. Peter A. Pyhrr, "Operational Auditing: A Run for Daylight," *Financial Executive* (May 1969), p. 19.

34. Lindberg and Cohn, *Operations Auditing*, p. 8.

35. Ibid., p. 5.

36. Santocki, "Management Audit," p. 15.

37. Lindberg and Cohn, *Operations Auditing*, p. 6.

38. Ibid., pp. 35-36.

39. Ibid., p. 36.

40. Ibid., p. 42.

41. Ibid., p. 10.

42. William B. Haase, "Cooperation Makes the Difference," *The Internal Auditor* XXX (July-August 1973), p. 43.

43. Malcolm S. Forbes, "Fact and Comment," *Forbes* CXIV (October 1, 1974), p. 18.

44. Lindberg and Cohn, *Operations Auditing*, p. 15.

45. Neil Doppelt, "Operational Auditing and the Management Letter," *Journal of Accountancy* CXXXIII (August 1971), p. 80.

46. Evans, op. cit., p. 47.

Notes to Chapter 3
Hospital Accounting and Auditing

1. A.C. Bachmeyer, F.E. Chapman, and John Bresnahan, "Hospital Accounting," *Modern Hospital* XIX (August 1922), p. 130.

2. Ibid. "Copyright 1922 figures by McGraw-Hill, Inc. Reprinted by permission from *Modern Hospital*, vol. XIX, no. 2 (August 1922). All rights reserved."

3. Ibid., p. 131.

4. Ibid.

5. Ibid., p. 130.

6. C. Rufus Rorem, "Cost Analysis for Hospitals," *Accounting Review* V (June 1930), p. 159.

7. C. Rufus Rorem, "Uniform Hospital Accounting," *Accounting Review* XI (June 1936), p. 158.

8. Ibid., p. 159.

9. Ibid., p. 160.

10. Ibid.

11. Ibid.

12. Ibid., p. 161.

13. Frederick Grubel, "Practical Aspects of Accounting and Auditing in Hospitals," *New York Certified Public Accountant* XXIV (June 1954), p. 382.

14. Ibid., p. 380.

15. Robert M. Sloane and Beverly LeBov Sloane, *A Guide to Health Facilities Personnel and Management* (St. Louis: C.V. Mosby Co., 1971), p. 84.

16. Philip Taylor and Benjamin O. Nelson, *Management Accounting for Hospitals* (Philadelphia: W.B. Saunders Company, 1964), p. 45.

17. Albert L. Craven, "Impact of Cost Finding Requirements of Medicare Legislation on Hospital Accounting and Cost Control," unpublished Ph.D. dissertation, Department of Accounting, University of Alabama, p. 57.

18. Ibid., p. 128.

19. *Chart of Accounts for Hospitals* (Chicago: American Hospital Association, 1966), p. 14.

20. Robert H. Montgomery, *Dicksee's Auditing* (New York: Ronald Press, 1909), p. 159.

21. *Hospital Audit Guide* (New York: American Institute of Certified Public Accountants, Inc., 1972), p. 3.

22. Ibid., p. 4.

23. *Audit Program for Hospitals Under the Health Insurance for the Aged Act Title XVIII* (Washington, D.C.: Social Security Administration, 1967), p. 3.

24. Craven, "Impact of Cost Finding Requirements," p. 47.

25. B. Saunders Midyette, "Operational Analysis: A New Internal Audit Concept," *Hospital Financial Management* XXIV (May 1970), p. 17.

26. Richard J. Wingard, "An Outside Audit Made a Good Charge System Better," *Hospitals* XXXIX (February 16, 1965), p. 68.

27. Thomas A. Blumenthal, "Management Review Program Develops 'In-Depth' Evaluations," *Hospitals* XLII (July 16, 1968), p. 92.

Notes to Chapter 4
Development of an Operations Audit Model

1. John W. Cook, "Operations Auditing," paper presented at 7th Annual Seminar, Trends in the Education of Accountants," Blacksburg, Virginia, November 15, 1974.

2. Roy A. Lindberg and Theodore Cohn, *Operations Auditing* (New York: American Management Association, 1972), p. 36.

3. Felix Pomeranz, "Communications—Raw Material of the Operational Audit," *Internal Auditor* XVIII (Winter 1961), p. 23.

4. Ronald S. Brown, CPA, "The Operational Audit," *The Lester Witte Report* V (Number 4, 1974), p. 2.

5. Ibid.

6. Robert R. Ringwood, "Operational Auditing for Government Programs," *International Journal of Government Auditing* I (January 1974), p. 13.

7. Lindberg and Cohn, *Operations Auditing*, p. 65.

8. George R. Terry, *Principles of Management*, 4th ed. (Homewood, Ill.: Richard D. Irwin, 1964), p. 454.

9. *HAS Guide for Uniform Reporting* (Chicago: American Hospital Association, 1972).

10. Interview with Oscar Momberger, American Hospital Association, August 15, 1974.

11. Lindberg and Cohn, *Operations Auditing*, p. 39.

12. Interview with Roy S. Yeatts, Assistant Controller, Watauga County Hospital, Boone, North Carolina, September 26, 1974.

13. Gerald Hewitt, "Innovations in Hospital Admissions," speech before the Hospital Financial Managers Association, Boone, North Carolina, August 15, 1974.

14. Letter and report from Vernon H. Blick, III, Patient Accounts Manager, Mercy Hospital, Charlotte, North Carolina, April 15, 1975.

15. Lindberg and Cohn, *Operations Auditing*, p. 35.

Notes to Chapter 5
Model In-Depth Audits

1. John H. Milsim, Efraim Turban, and Ilan Vertinsky, "Hospital Admission Systems: Their Evaluation and Management," *Management Science* XIX (February 1973), p. 646-66.

2. George R. Terry, *Principles of Management*, 4th ed. (Homewood, Ill.: Richard D. Irwin, 1964), p. 278.

3. Milsim et al., "Hospital Admission Systems."

4. Terry, *Principles of Management*, p. 743.

5. "6 Point Program to Implement Now Before Unionization Drives Begin," *Hospital Financial Management* XXVIII (November 1974), p. 23.

6. *Statement on Auditing Standards* (New York: American Institute of Certified Public Accountants, Inc., 1973), p. 13.

Bibliography

Bibliography

Books and Reports

Anthony, Robert N. and Hekimian, James S. *Operations Cost Control.* Homewood, Ill.: Richard D. Irwin, 1967.
Auditing Standards and Procedures, Statements on Auditing Standards No. 33. New York: American Institute of Certified Public Accountants, Inc., 1963.
Berki, Sylvester E. *Hospital Economics.* Lexington, Mass.: D.C. Heath, 1972.
Budgeting Procedures for Hospitals. Chicago: American Hospital Association, 1971.
Case Studies Seminar on Sophisticated Auditing Techniques. Washington: Federal Government Accountants Association, 1974.
Cashin, James A., ed. *Handbook for Auditors.* New York: McGraw-Hill, 1971.
Chart of Accounts for Hospitals. Chicago: American Hospital Association, 1966.
Cost Allocation Program: Management Reports. Chicago: American Hospital Association, 1974.
Discharge Planning for Hospitals. Chicago: American Hospital Association, 1974.
Durbin, Richard L. and Springall, W. Herbert. *Organization and Administration of Health Care: Theory, Practice, Environment.* St. Louis: C.V. Mosby Company, 1969.
England, Wilbur B. *The Purchasing System.* Homewood, Ill.: Richard D. Irwin, 1967.
Examples of Findings from Government Audits. Washington, D.C.: U.S. Government Printing Office, 1973.
Griffith, John R. *Quantitative Techniques for Hospital Planning and Control.* Lexington, Mass.: D.C. Heath, 1972.
HAS Six Month National Comparison for Period Ending December 31, 1972. Chicago: American Hospital Association, 1973.
Heckert, J. Brooks and Wilson, James D. *Controllership.* New York: Ronald Press, 1963.
Henke, Emerson O. *Accounting for Nonprofit Organizations.* Belmont, Calif.: Wadsworth, 1966.
Hepner, James O., Boyer, John M., and Westerhaus, Carl L. *Personnel Administration and Labor Relations in Health Care Facilities.* St. Louis, C.V. Mosby Company, 1969.
Heydebrand, Wolf. *Hospital Bureaucracy.* New York: Dunellen, 1973.
Holmes, Arthur W. and Overmyer, Wayne S. *Auditing Principles and Procedures.* Homewood, Ill.: Richard D. Irwin, 1971.
HAS Guide for Uniform Reporting. Chicago: American Hospital Association, 1972.
Hospital Audit Guide. New York: American Institute of Certified Public Accountants, Inc., 1972.

Illinois Use of Public Accountants for Auditing State Activities. Washington, D.C.: U.S. Government Printing Office, 1973.

Internal Auditing, Studies in Business Policy, No. 111. New York: National Industrial Conference Board, 1963.

Lindberg, Roy A. and Cohn, Theodore. *Operations Auditing.* New York: American Management Association, 1972.

Livingstone, John Leslie and Gunn, Sanford C. *Accounting for Social Goals: Budgeting and Analysis of Nonmarket Projects.* New York: Harper and Row, 1974.

Mautz, R.K. and Sharaf, Hussein A. *The Philosophy of Auditing.* Evanston, Ill.: American Accounting Association, 1961.

McGibony, John R. *Principles of Hospital Administration,* 2nd ed. New York: G.P. Putnam's Sons, 1969.

Sawyer, Lawrence B. *Modern Internal Auditing.* Orlando, Fla.: Institute of Internal Auditors, 1973.

Somers, Anne R. *Health Care in Transition: Directions for the Future.* Chicago: Hospital Research and Educational Trust, 1971.

Standards for Audit of Governmental Organizations, Programs, Activities and Functions. Washington, D.C.: U.S. Government Printing Office, 1974.

Statement of Responsibilities of the Internal Auditor. Orlando, Fla.: Institute of Internal Auditors, 1957.

Stettler, Howard F. *Systems Based Independent Audits,* 2nd ed. Englewood Cliffs, N.J.: Prentice-Hall, 1974.

Taylor, Phillip and Nelson, Benjamin O. *Management Accounting for Hospitals.* Philadelphia: W.B. Saunders Co., 1964.

Periodicals

Andrews, Frederick B. "Compulsory Audit of Corporations," *Journal of Accountancy* LIV (November 1932), pp. 352ff.

Bachmeyer, A.C., Chapman, F.E., and Bresnahan, John. "Hospital Accounting," *Modern Hospital* XIX (August, 1922), pp. 130-31.

Blough, Carmen G. "Plant Fund Accounting in Hospital Case Study," *Journal of Accountancy* CIII (April 1957), pp. 73-74.

Brown, Ronald S. "The Operational Audit," *Lester Witte Report* V, No. 4 (1974), pp. 1-2.

Brown, R. Gene. "Changing Audit Objectives and Techniques," *Accounting Review* XXXVII (October 1962), pp. 696-99.

Burton, John C. "Management Auditing," *Journal of Accountancy* CXXV (May 1968), pp. 41-46.

Churchill, Neil C. and Cyert, Richard M. "An Experiment in Management Auditing," *Journal of Accountancy* CXXI (February 1966), pp. 39-43.

Dewitt, Frank. "Measuring Management Performance," *Management Accounting* LIV (November 1972), pp. 18-22.

Dodwell, Joseph W. "Operational Auditing: A Part of the Basic Audit," *Journal of Accountancy* CXXI (June 1966), pp. 31-39.

Doppelt, Neil. "Operational Auditing and the Management Letter," *Journal of Accountancy* CXXXII (August 1971), pp. 82-83.

Estes, Ralph. "A Comprehensive Corporate Social Reporting Model," *Federal Accountant* XXIII (December 1974), pp. 9-19.

Evans, E.R. "Approach: The Key to Operational Auditing," *The Internal Auditor* XXII (Spring 1966), pp. 29-36.

Evans, E.R. "Some Benefits of Operational Auditing," *The Internal Auditor* XXVI (March-April 1969), pp. 47ff.

"Fast Responses to Health Care Problems," *E and E* (Summer 1974), pp. 10-17.

Ferderber, Charles J. "Give Your Hospital a Formal Set of Policies and Procedures," *Hospital Financial Management* XXVII (April 1973), pp. 47ff.

Goodfellow, Matthew. "Keeping Your Employees' Morale Up Takes More Than Money," *Hospital Financial Management* XXVIII (November 1974), pp. 24-29.

Grubel, Frederick. "Practical Aspects of Accounting and Auditing in Hospitals," *New York Certified Public Accountant* XXIV (June 1954), pp. 379-84.

Haase, William B. "Cooperation Makes the Difference," *The Internal Auditor* XXX (July-August 1973), pp. 43ff.

Henke, Emerson O. "Audit Reports for Not-for-Profit Organizations," *Texas CPA* (April 1972), pp. 20-24.

Hilliard, Hugh E. "Management's View of Audits," *Hospital Financial Management* XXIV (November 1970), pp. 12ff.

Jenkins, S.R. "The Management Audit: A Challenge for the Practitioner," *Accountants' Journal* LII (August 1973), pp. 18-21.

Langenderfer, Harold Q. and Robertson, Jack C. "A Theoretical Structure for Independent Audits of Management," *Accounting Review* XLIV (October 1969), pp. 777-87.

Lindberg, Roy. "Operations Auditing: What It Is, What It Isn't," *Management Review* LVIII (December 1969), pp. 2-10.

Lublin, Joann S. "Outfit That Accredits Hospitals Helps Set Quality of Patient Care," *Wall Street Journal* (January 13, 1975), pp. 1ff.

Melloan, George. "Inside Auditors Widen Role as 'Eyes and Ears' for Top Management," *Wall Street Journal* (October 26, 1964), pp. 1ff.

Meyers, E.B. "Operational Auditing," *The Internal Auditor* XXIII (Winter 1966), pp. 17-24.

Milsim, John H., Turban, Efraim, and Vertinsky, Ilan. "Hospital Admission Systems: Their Evolution and Management," *Management Science* XIX (February 1973), pp. 646-66.

Minkin, Max. "Some New Paths to Program Evaluation Review," *Federal Accountant* XXIII (March 1974), pp. 51-55.

Morin, Desmond. "The Operational Audit," *International Journal of Government Auditing* I (January 1974), pp. 12-13.

Morse, Ellsworth H., Jr. "Comments on Survey of Attitudes on Management Auditing," *Accounting Review* XLVIII (January 1973), pp. 120-22.

———. "Performance and Operational Auditing," *Journal of Accountancy* CXXXI (June 1971), pp. 45-46.

Murphy, Thomas, Jr. "The Hospital Treasurer and Controller: Duties and Responsibilities," *Hospital Financial Management* LXVIII (April 1970), pp. 11-14.

Norgaard, Corinne T. "Operational Auditing: A Part of the Control Process," *Management Accounting* LIII (March 1972), pp. 25-28.

———. "The Professional Accountant's View of Operational Auditing," *Journal of Accountancy* CXXVIII (December 1969), pp. 45-48.

Ostrander, Forst R. "How a Management Audit Helped One Hospital," *Hospital Management* LXVIII (July 1949), pp. 88-90.

Oviatt, Bill. "Payment Patterns," *Hospital Financial Management* XXVIII (November 1974), p. 48.

Petrick, M.B. "Self-Pay Collections Improved With Bank Loan Plan," *Hospital Financial Management* XXVIII (September 1974), pp. 42-45.

Pointer, Larry Gene. "Internal Auditing Comes of Age," *The Internal Auditor* XXX (September-October 1973), pp. 35ff.

Pomeranz, Felix. "Communications—Raw Material of the Operational Audit," *The Internal Auditor* XVIII (Winter 1961), 16-26.

Pyhrr, Peter A. "Operational Auditing: A Run for Daylight," *Financial Executive* (May 1969), pp. 19ff.

Quinn, John P. "The AICPA Audit Guide Can Help You Make Your Financial Statements Communicate," *Hospital Financial Management* XXVII (May 1973), pp. 69ff.

———. "Financial Reporting for Voluntary Hospitals," *Price Waterhouse Review* (Summer 1970), pp. 20-29.

Rea, George and Peper, John L. "Establishing a Control Over Hospital Income," *N.A.C.A. Bulletin* (January 15, 1935), pp. 556-61.

"Report of the Committee on Basic Auditing Concepts," *Accounting Review* XLVII (Supplement, 1972), pp. 15-74.

Ringwood, Robert R. "Operational Auditing for Government Programs," *International Journal of Government Auditing* I (January 1974), pp. 2-3.

Roth, J.L. "What's Ahead for the Auditors," *Journal of Accountancy* CXXVII (December 1967), pp. 60-62.

Santocki, J. "Management Audit: Chance, Challenge, or Lost Opportunity," *The Accountant* CLXX (January 3, 1974), pp. 14-18.

Sawyer, Lawrence B. "Just What Is Management Auditing," *The Internal Auditor* XXX (March-April 1973), pp. 10-21.

Schneider, Aaron. "What Operational Auditing Is—And Isn't," *The Internal Auditor* XXX (September-October 1973), pp. 10-19.

Schulte, Arthur A. "Compatibility of Management Consulting and Auditing," *Accounting Review* XL (July 1965), pp. 587-93.

Smith, Charles H., Lanier, Roy A., and Taylor, Martin E. "The Need for and Scope of the Audit of Management: A Survey of Attitudes," *Accounting Review* SLVII (April 1972), pp. 270-83.

Smith, Charles H. and Lanier, Roy A. "The Audit of Management: Report on a Field Study," *Management Accounting* LI (June 1970), pp. 24ff.

Steven, Anton. "Operational Audits of Construction Contracts," *The Internal Auditor* XXX (September-October 1973), pp. 10ff.

Tower, Ralph B. "Hospital Accounting and the CPA," *Florida CPA* (July 1974), pp. 41-45.

Wasser, Max. "The Independent Auditor's Role in Charitable Organizations," *New York Certified Public Accountant* (June 1954), pp. 374-78.

Wingard, Richard J. "An Outside Audit Made a Good Charge System Better," *Hospitals* XXIX (February 16, 1965), pp. 68-71.

Unpublished Materials

Bomeli, Edwin Clarence. "The Audit of Management Performance." Unpublished Ph.D. dissertation, Department of Accounting and Finance, Michigan State University, 1963.

Cook, John W. "Operational Auditing." Paper delivered at the meeting of the Seventh Annual Seminar, "Trends in the Education of Accountants," Blacksburg, Virginia, November 15, 1974.

Craven, Albert L. "Impact of Cost Finding Requirements of Medicare Legislation on Hospital Accounting and Cost Control." Unpublished Ph.D. dissertation, Department of Accounting, University of Alabama, 1968.

Denis, Robert Bassett. "A Critical Study of Operations Auditing." Unpublished Ph.D. dissertation, Department of Accounting, American University, 1972.

Jones, R.H. "Audit of the Future." Paper delivered at the meeting of the New York City chapter of the Institute of Internal Auditors, February 6, 1969.

Lahey, James Montgomery. "Evolution of the Concept of an Audit in Authoritative Professional Literature." Unpublished Ph.D. dissertation, Department of Accounting, University of Illinois, 1969.

Lindquist, Stanton C. "A Search for Practical Evaluation Standards for Use by Certified Public Accountants in Conducting Management Audits." Unpublished Ph.D. dissertation, Department of Business Administration, University of Missouri, 1972.

Nicol, Robert Edward George. "An Inquiry into the Problems of Definition and Measurement in Operational Auditing by Professional Accountants." Unpublished Ph.D. dissertation, Department of Business Administration, University of California at Los Angeles, 1969.

U.S. Atomic Energy Commission—Oak Ridge Operations. "Methodology of Operational Auditing." Oak Ridge, Tennessee, 1974. (Mimeographed.)

Interviews

Hewitt, Gerald N., Vice President-Professional and Financial Services, North Carolina Baptist Hospital, Winston-Salem, North Carolina, August 15, 1974.

Knight, Meredith, Controller, Watauga County Hospital, Boone, North Carolina, August 15, 1974.

Momberger, Oscar J., Division of Hospital Administrative Services, American Hospital Association, Mooresville, North Carolina, August 14, 1974.

Rinnie, Allen, Assistant Director, North Carolina Hospital Association, Raleigh, North Carolina, August 14, 1974.

Yeatts, Roy S., Assistant Controller, Watauga County Hospital, Boone, North Carolina, August 15, 1974.

Index

accounting, 21; department, 56-59; questionnaire, 85-90
admissions, 51-54
American Hospital Association, 21, 26, 28
AICPA, 8, 26
auditing, 7-13; compliance, 12; economy, 13; history, 7-9; internal, 9-13; philosophy, 31
audit report, 2, 5, 46, 110, 112; final report, 17; preliminary report, 16; special purposes, 8

budgets, 38; accounting, 57; patient census management, 53

CPA firms, 2-3, 18
consultants, 18-19
cost reimbursement, 25

depreciation, 23
discharges, 6, 51-54

financial analysis, 42-45
flow charts, 38

General Accounting Office, 2, 12, 13
goals, 37

HAS reports, 38, 42; sample, 113-116

in-depth audit, 17, 46
Institute of Internal Auditors, 10
internal audits, 9-13; history, 9; objectives, 11
internal control, 57; payroll, 59
interviews, 46, 52; management, 39; questionnaire, 40

job descriptions, 37

managerial audit. *See* operations audit
Medicare, 26-27
minutes of meetings, 38

National Industrial Conference Board, 11
1933 Committee Report, 23
nonprofit hospital, 3, 3n

observation, 17
operations audit, 2, 28; in-depth stage, 17-46; limitations, 18; objectives, 13-16; preliminary stage, 16; program, 68; sources of data, 16, 32, 49
operations audit model, 5-6, 31-51
organization charts, 37

patient census management, 51-54; questionnaire, 73-78
patient mix, 51
payroll department, 59-61; questionnaire, 59, 91-95
personnel department, 54-56; questionnaire, 79-84
physical tour, 32-36; questionnaire, 33-36
preliminary audit, 16, 32
procedures manuals, 37; accounting, 58; patient census management, 52; payroll, 59; purchasing, 62; receiving and materials handling, 65
purchasing, 61-64; questionnaire, 61, 97-101

questionnaires, 17, 40, 52; accounting, 85-90; patient census management, 73-78; payroll, 91-95; personnel, 79-84; purchasing, 97-101; receiving and materials handling, 103-107

receiving and materials handling, 64-66; questionnaire, 103-107

social accounting, 67
survey memorandum, 16, 45-46, 109, 111

written data, 36

About the Author

Dale L. Flesher is assistant professor of accounting at Appalachian State University in Boone, North Carolina. He received the bachelor's and master's degrees from Ball State University in Muncie, Indiana, and the Ph.D. from the University of Cincinnati. Dr. Flesher is a Certified Public Accountant with experience in both public and industrial accounting. He is also a holder of the new Certificate in Management Accounting. On this latter exam, Dr. Flesher received the Certificate of Distinguished Performance for achieving one of the ten highest scores in the nation. Dr. Flesher has authored numerous articles for accounting journals. He is a member of the National Association of Accountants, the American Accounting Association, the Academy of Accounting Historians, the Institute of Management Accounting, and the North Carolina Association of Certified Public Accountants.

Related Lexington Books

Ammer, Dean S., *Purchasing and Materials Management*, 192 pp., 1975
Berger, Laurence B., Sullivan, Paul R., *Measuring Hospital Inflation*, 256 pp., 1975
Berki, Sylvester E., *Hospital Economics*, 288 pp., 1972
Griffith, John R., *Quantitative Techniques for Hospital Planning and Control*, 308 pp., 1973
Dowling, William L., *The Analysis of Hospital Production*, In Press